Women and Security Governance in Africa

Through the voices of the peoples of Africa and the global South, Pambazuka Press and Pambazuka News disseminate analysis and debate on the struggle for freedom and justice.

Pambazuka Press – www.pambazukapress.org

 A Pan-African publisher of progressive books and DVDs on Africa and the global South that aim to stimulate discussion, analysis and engagement. Our publications address issues of human rights, social justice, advocacy, the politics of aid, development and international finance, women's rights, emerging powers and activism. They are primarily written by well-known African academics and activists. All books are available as ebooks.

Pambazuka News – www.pambazuka.org

 The award-winning and influential electronic weekly newsletter providing a platform for progressive Pan-African perspectives on politics, development and global affairs. With more than 2,500 contributors across the continent and a readership of more than 660,000, Pambazuka News has become the indispensable source of authentic voices of Africa's social analysts and activists.

Pambazuka Press and Pambazuka News are published by Fahamu (www.fahamu.org)

Women and Security Governance in Africa

Edited by 'Funmi Olonisakin
and Awino Okech

Pambazuka Press
An imprint of Fahamu

Published 2011 by Pambazuka Press, an imprint of Fahamu
Cape Town, Dakar, Nairobi and Oxford
www.pambazukapress.org www.fahamubooks.org www.pambazuka.org

Fahamu, 2nd floor, 51 Cornmarket Street, Oxford OX1 3HA, UK
Fahamu Kenya, PO Box 47158, 00100 GPO, Nairobi, Kenya
Fahamu Senegal, 9 Cité Sonatel 2, POB 25021, Dakar-Fann, Dakar, Senegal
Fahamu South Africa, c/o 19 Nerina Crescent, Fish Hoek,
7975 Cape Town, South Africa

Pambazuka Press wishes to thank the African Women's Development Fund
for their support for the publication and distribution of this book

First published 2011

British Library Cataloguing in Publication Data
A catalogue record for this book is available from the British Library

ISBN: 978-1-906387-89-1 paperback
ISBN: 978-1-906387-90-7 ebook – pdf

Printed by National Printing Press, Bangalore, India

Africa is the only place where many Africans
do not say 'our government', we say 'the government'.
It is only on this continent, when you are in trouble
you do not run to the police, you run away from the police.
Tajudeen Abdul-Raheem
....

To the memory of Tajudeen Abdul-Raheem,
a Pan-African scholar and activist who dedicated
his life to the campaign for an Africa of free,
equal and dignified citizens

Contents

Abbreviations

AU	African Union
AFELL	Association of Female Lawyers of Liberia
AFL	Armed Forces of Liberia
AFRC	Armed Forces Revolutionary Council
AFRICOM	United States African Command
AMISOM	AU Mission in Somalia
ANC	African National Congress
ASF	African Standby Force
ASSN	Africa Security Sector Network
AWDF	African Women's Development Fund
BIN	Bureau of Immigration and Naturalisation (Liberia)
CAR	Central African Republic
CDF	Civil Defence Forces (Sierra Leone)
CSO	civil society organisation
CPA	Comprehensive Peace Agreement (Liberia)
CSDG	Conflict, Security and Development Group
DRC	Democratic Republic of Congo
DCAF	Geneva Centre for Democratic Control of Armed Forces
DDR	disarmament, demobilisation and reintegration
EASBRIG	East African Standby Brigade
ECOWAS	Economic Community of West African States
ECOMIL	ECOWAS Mission in Liberia
ECOMOG	ECOWAS Ceasefire Monitoring Group
ECPF	ECOWAS Conflict Prevention Framework
FAS	Femmes Africa Solidarité
FEMNET	African Women's Development and Communications Network
Frelimo	Frente de Libertação de Moçambique
GPA	General Peace Agreement (Mozambique)
ICC	International Criminal Court
ICTJ	International Centre for Transitional Justice
IDP	internally displaced person
IER	Instance Equité et Réconciliation
IGAD	Intergovernmental Authority on Development

LNP	Liberia National Police
LURD	Liberians United for Reconciliation and Democracy
LWI	Liberian Women's Initiative
MARWOPNET	Mano River Women's Peace Network
MSWGCA	Ministry of Social Welfare, Gender and Children's Affairs (Sierra Leone)
NaCSA	National Commission for Social Action
NGO	non-governmental organisation
NPFL	National Patriotic Front of Liberia
OAU	Organisation of African Unity
ONUMOZ	United Nations Operations in Mozambique
PCRDPF	Post-conflict Reconstruction and Development Policy Framework (of the African Union)
PSC	Peace and Security Council (of the African Union)
Renamo	Resistência Nacional Moçambicana
RUF/SL	Revolutionary United Front of Sierra Leone
SADC	Southern African Development Community
SCSL	Special Court for Sierra Leone
SGBV	sexual and gender-based violence
SSR	security sector reform
TRC	Truth and Reconciliation Commission
UNAMID	AU/UN Joint Hybrid Operation in Darfur
UNAMSIL	United Nations Mission to Sierra Leone
Unesco	United Nations Educational, Scientific and Cultural Organization
UNHCR	United Nations High Commissioner for Refugees
UNIFEM	United Nations Development Fund for Women
UNMIL	United Nations Mission in Liberia
UNPBF	United Nations Peace Building Fund
UNSC	United Nations Security Council
WACSOF	West Africa Civil Society Forum
WIPNET	Women in Peacebuilding Network
WIPSEN-Africa	Women Peace and Security Network Africa
WPS	Women Peace and Security
ZANU	Zimbabwe African National Union

Preface

'Funmi Olonisakin and Awino Okech

This book is the result of a meeting of minds among a group of scholars and activists working on a range of African security and development issues; it flows from their commitment to providing an intellectual response to critical gaps in the provision and governance of security in Africa.

Two observations informed this response. The first is that despite the proliferation of policy instruments and programmes dedicated to the promotion of gender equality in the field of peace and security, women's security concerns are rarely a priority on security agendas. Second, and in the same vein, there is a growing number of women's groups advocating the inclusion of women's security concerns particularly in situations of armed conflict, but women are hardly represented in security decision-making processes whether at national or regional levels.

The question therefore arises as to why policies and campaigns for the inclusion of women's security concerns and their participation in security decision making are far removed from the actual security decision-making processes in varying contexts. Are these two separate and unrelated agendas? Or is there a deeper structural factor that makes it difficult for women's concerns to be accommodated within the larger security discourse? Are women alone in experiencing this separation or exclusion from mainstream security decision making?

In response to these questions, this volume interrogates the structures and processes that guide security governance across a number of national contexts and at continental and regional levels. There are a variety of national contexts in which a semblance of security reform and governance takes place in Africa and that can potentially offer useful lessons. One of these is the transition from long-term authoritarian rule to more participatory systems of governance. Others concern post-conflict situations and transitions from armed conflict to stable peace.

In this book, we focus on a small sample of conflict and post-conflict transitions, and also draw from processes and experiences of the African Union (AU) and the Economic Community of West African States (ECOWAS). We found conflict-affected environments particularly attractive because of the opportunities they offer for comprehensive governance reform and a chance to examine these processes. The regional norm-setting processes in West Africa, which were catalysed by the ECOWAS intervention in the armed conflicts in Liberia and Sierra Leone, and the African Union's peace and security architecture also offer important insights about the challenges of guaranteeing security for African states and societies.

The completion of this book was made possible with the support and collaboration of a number of people. First and foremost, we would like to thank the authors for their commitment to meeting the tight deadlines and especially for their contributions, from which we gained a great deal of insight. We would also like to acknowledge the African Women's Development Fund (AWDF) and the African Leadership Centre through the Conflict Security and Development Group (CSDG), King's College London, for co-sponsoring this volume. Our thanks also go to Pambazuka Press for its foresight in recognising the importance of the reflections contained in this book.

The rapid increase in security governance initiatives and the concomitant development of women and security as a field of interest on the African continent, in both academic and policy circles, makes this book timely. We hope that it will make a significant contribution to the understanding among specialists and observers alike of the relevance of security governance debates in Africa and particularly, but not exclusively, of how a women's rights discourse can contribute to transforming approaches.

Introduction

'Funmi Olonisakin and Awino Okech

As recently as 20 years ago, the subject of security governance and its centrality to development was not open to much debate. In Africa, the notion of security governance was not discussed outside of governments and their appointed agents. It did not include civil society, let alone women's rights analysts and actors, nor was the role of women in the processes and structures of security governance accorded space in policy planning and related dialogues. The defence and security of the African state was the sole focus of the security discourse and in that context, the security concerns of citizens rarely featured. Two decades later, security and development has become the focus of the World Bank's 2011 *World Development Report* (WDR). This is in part the result of more than two decades of debate about people-centred security (human security) vis-à-vis the defence and security of the state.

In the period since the end of the cold war, the world has come to embrace the notion that people ought to be the reference point in security discourse and planning. Africa has provided much of the empirical evidence that led to the treatment, in policy circles, of security and development as two sides of the same coin, given the varying manifestations of governance deficits and insecurity in the region. The idea that the concerns of women should be accorded a place in that discourse has also been 'generally accepted'. But beyond this, the discussion of the role of women in peace and security has evolved separately and not as an integral part of the security governance debate.

When United Nations Security Council Resolution 1325 on women, peace and security was adopted in October 2000, it was hailed by policy analysts and international observers alike as a hallmark instrument. It was the first time that the security concerns

1

of women in situations of armed conflict and their role in peace building had been placed on the agenda of the UN Security Council. Ten years after the adoption of this resolution, it has yet to make a substantial practical difference in the very societies and regions where women remain disproportionately affected by armed conflict and grossly under-represented in peace processes. This realisation, in part, led to the adoption in 2008 and 2009 of three other Security Council resolutions. Resolution 1820 focuses on sexual violence in conflict, while 1889, which proposes the appointment of a special representative on violence against women, also focuses on strengthening reporting, prevention and response mechanisms. Resolution 1889 calls for the development of indicators to measure progress in addressing women, peace and security issues by March 2010. Not surprisingly, the slow uptake of the provisions of Resolution 1325 on the ground in Africa in particular means that there has been no real grasp of the linkage between the women's security agenda and the governance of security as a whole.

The general separation of the women's agenda from the security governance agenda raises a number of important questions about the depth and applicability of seemingly new and transformational security paradigms. In this regard, two sets of questions are considered in this volume. First, to what extent does the emerging people-centred security agenda apply to all citizens equally within a state's boundaries? How real and how universally applicable is the notion and agenda of a people-centred approach to security? Whose narrative of security is dominant? Who and what determine who and what is secured? Second, is stable peace and development attainable without inclusive security? What governance arrangements can ensure inclusive security? How does this vary from one context to another?

This book examines the nature and scope of security governance discourse in varying contexts in Africa and assesses to what extent this converges with women's security concerns and aspirations. The volume is guided by a central thesis: that the extent to which women's agendas are visible in security governance arrangements is a reflection of a society's realisation (or not) of a people-centred and inclusive security. Following from this, we argue that such convergence is possible only with a security agenda that is organically driven and necessarily built on the narratives of the affected communities. It offers a critique of African and international approaches to the security and development challenges of Africa. The book proceeds from the point that policy and practice in this regard are dominated by global actors in connivance with an African elite, largely to the exclusion of African citizens and legitimate non-state actors; the women's security agenda is further marginal to the agenda of non-state actors.

Arguing that the security narratives transferred from extra-African sources do not bear much resemblance to the security needs of the vast majority of Africans, not least women, the book offers alternative narratives of security in Africa. Women's security narratives are particularly significant in this regard because they point to fundamental gaps not only in the security frameworks of African states and regional security institutions, but also because understanding them offers a fresh inroad into how to transform security governance for the benefit of all and not just a few Africans.

This book questions the assumptions which guide security governance and attempts to explain why women's narratives and their needs are often missing from the discourse. We locate feminist analysis, and its contribution to challenging the dominant paradigms which have shaped the security discourse, by questioning the ability, and legitimacy, of external actors to bring about gender-related structural changes in the way the security establishment is governed in Africa. We attempt to provide a more robust narrative that substantively identifies new gendered and inclusive approaches to security governance discourse. Filling these crucial knowledge gaps will therefore present African citizens and civil society actors with an equally daunting but perhaps more manageable challenge. This is to shape a strategy for engaging critical institutions and actors nationally, regionally and globally so that they can become more responsive to citizens' security concerns and to do so from a basis of equity.

This book draws on four key themes. The first focuses on security as a contextual and gendered concept. The second concerns the structures of security governance at regional levels. The third deals with security governance and reform in post-conflict environments while the fourth and last focuses on transitional justice and its intersection with security governance.

To this end the chapters in this book are divided into three parts. Part 1 offers a conceptual understanding of security governance within three frameworks. The first framework locates security governance as an evolving discourse within the domain of international relations and national or state security arrangements. The second reflects on transitional justice processes as a zone within which security sector reform projects across the continent have been undertaken while the third offers a feminist critique of this security governance, locating the role of women in the African state and examining the centrality of body politics as an inroad to understanding insecurity.

The first chapter of Part 1 traces the trajectory of security discourse on the continent. 'Funmi Olonisakin examines the emergence and embedding of state-centric security frameworks. This is in part an inheritance from a colonial legacy of state formation that shaped the ideas of insecurity largely in terms of external aggressors and the need to secure state borders. She goes on to examine the emergence of what she describes as the new security narratives: an expanded notion of security that recognises the role of non-state actors as well as other facets of what constitutes security. She interrogates the extent to which the changing narratives over time, developments in the international community and the introduction of new actors have transformed security governance to the benefit of women.

In Chapter 2, Comfort Ero continues along this line by examining the nature of security sector reform within transitional contexts and as part of transitional justice frameworks. She brings to the foreground the need for a reflective approach that questions:

> [H]ow real are the opportunities in the transitional contexts for setting a transformative agenda in ways that include a women's agenda? Preventing the recurrence of human rights violations and promoting social reconstruction as well as the rule of law are key objectives of transitional justice. In pursuing these objectives, what spaces are created and what gains have emerged to bring to the fore a gendered perspective that impacts on post-conflict governance in general?

In providing a rich engagement with examples of transitional justice processes (Morroco, Sierra Leone and Liberia) and how they have taken on board concerns central to women, Ero flags a number of gaps. She highlights the need to engage with structural questions. This requires holistic strategies that take into account the very principles on which the state is founded. Borrowing Hamber et al's (2006) concept of re-imagining security, she highlights the need for alternative discourses to those that currently shape security governance approaches. She notes that these must of necessity grapple with how to centralise the already rich empirical data (the skills and experiences of women). She concludes by noting the need for transitional justice projects that include security sector governance to engage in redistributive justice and not just retributive or restorative justice. She asserts the need for such projects to engage with the mechanisms to transform pre-existing structural inequalities even if it is by highlighting how these remain entrenched in the transitioning state.

Awino Okech builds on this conversation in Chapter 3 by locating women within the state in Africa through highlighting the terms on which women have been part of the state and nation-building process. She argues that this process entrenched approaches that seek to maintain power over women. Situating body politics and sexuality as a paradigm, Okech argues that the debates around the strategic and systematic use of violence against women during situations of armed conflict are part of state-building processes that emphasise the need for purity, control and the maintenance of definitive borders. The deployment of women as border guards cannot be discounted and as such engagement by women's rights activists in security governance transformation must not only take account of the gendered experiences of conflict in terms of who suffers more 'harm', but must also engage with why this violence is meted out in this manner in the first place. Moving away from a discourse that entrenches victimhood and reinforces the biological and reproductive functions of women as a means to negotiate for power, Okech situates feminist scholarship in the context of women and the nation state. She argues for one, the recognition of the destabilising nature of sexuality as a framework and the need to engage with this in more useful ways beyond current approaches that reinforce the fraught polarities

5

of male and female. She also calls for a rethinking of approaches to engaging states in Africa given the 'irrational' nature through which women have encountered this entity.

Part 2 of the book focuses on country-specific case studies that bring to bear the robust engagement of African women in conflict and post-conflict processes. In these environments, the opportunity is often created for a transformation in governance systems, the breakdown of which led to the outbreak of armed conflict in the first instance. There is often a real opportunity to situate women's security concerns within the new security governance arrangements. In Africa's post-conflict environments, women's security concerns are constantly intertwined with the need to seek justice for the various crimes against humanity committed during wartime. Ensuring complementary structures and processes of security governance and transitional justice has become a prime concern in these contexts.

Drawing on Liberia, Sierra Leone and Mozambique, the four authors in Part 2 highlight the complex arrangements involved in negotiating a space for women's engagement in the cessation of violence, peace agreements and in rebuilding the state. In Chapter 4 on Liberia, Ecoma Alaga offers a first-hand account as a practitioner and as founding member of the Women in Peacebuilding Network (WIPNET) that was central to the large-scale mobilisation of women in demanding peace. She examines the strategies deployed by the movement ideologically in grounding their work in Galtung's conflict transformation theories. Rooted in the realities of women, they mobilised as sisters, mothers and daughters across class and political affiliation and organisationally through the institution of membership cards and by using clothing as an identification mechanism. The now successful story of the WIPNET campaign in barricading the peace talks in Accra has since been immortalised in the film *Pray the Devil Back to Hell*. Alaga is quick to note the gains that emerged with the election of a new president in Liberia. She highlights the specific gender-related initiatives within the Liberian national police force that have included the provision of gender training for police personnel, the establishment of protection units for women and children within police stations, the deployment of an all-female Indian peacekeeping unit and the introduction of quotas together with definite enforcement mechanisms, such as the accelerated learning programme to increase female enrolment. At the level of the Liberian parliament, the presence of the national security strategy, which calls for gender mainstreaming within the security sector, was also adopted in 2008. This is in addition to the specialised parliamentary committees on defence and security that have also benefited from gender training provided by a range of civil society organisations.

While recognising that the women's peace activism campaign, which began at the height of the conflict (and continued long after the peace agreement was signed), has contributed to an expansion of political space for women in Liberia, she nonetheless notes that the post-war debates around security have not transformed gender relations nor mainstreamed women's issues. She attributes this to the separate evolution of the role of women in peace and security and the current security sector reform (SSR) process. She argues that the gender dimensions of SSR in Liberia have been institution specific rather than holistic, and even at this level any change has been ad hoc, fragmented and exclusive of the very women who are supposedly the beneficiaries. Alaga's concluding call is for the women's peace movement, which has fallen into a lull, to see in SSR opportunities to continue to infuse a change agenda and for the state to draw on the success of this movement.

Mohammed Sidi Bah's chapter on Sierra Leone (Chapter 5) draws on his first-hand experience as the former director of the body mandated by the Sierra Leone Truth and Reconciliation Commission (TRC) to coordinate reparations – the National Commission for Social Action (NaCSA). Bah emphasises concerns previously touched on by Ero, flagging the highly destabilising nature of transitional justice and the associated reform process in an extremely fragile state that is 90 per cent dependent on donor funding. The influence and role of the international community, and not just in the conflict and post-conflict arrangements, presents a particular dynamic. One of the terms under which the new state proceeds is framed by a blanket amnesty to perpetrators of sexual and gender-based violence under Article IX of the Lomé Peace Accord:

> To consolidate the peace and promote the cause of national reconciliation, the Government of Sierra Leone shall ensure that no official or judicial action is taken against any member of the RUF/SL, ex-AFRC, ex-SLA, or CDF in respect of anything done by them in pursuit of their objectives as members of those organisations.

This has happened in a context in which the processes that have subsequently centred on women's rights have largely been driven by international organisations and/or civil society actors who have notably been able to push through gender-sensitive bills and policies and have ensured the ratification and domestication of international instruments protecting women's rights. These include domesticating the principles of the Convention on the Elimination of all Forms of Discrimination Against Women (CEDAW), the African Union (AU) protocol on women's rights, the Beijing Platform for Action and the International Convention on Economic and Social Rights, United Nations Security Council (UNSC) Resolution 1325, the Rome Statute, and the United Nations High Commissioner for Refugees (UNHCR) guidelines on Sexual and Gender-based Violence against Refugees, Returnees and Displaced Persons. These international instruments are embodied in four pieces of gender legislation: the Domestic Violence Act 2007, the Devolution of Estate Act 2007, the Registration of Customary Marriages and Divorce Act 2007 and the Child Rights Act 2007.

Despite these efforts to bring Sierra Leone's national legislation into line with international obligations, Bah argues that the legal landscape is replete with contradictory and outdated legislation which negatively affects women's access to justice, although attempts are underway to reform or repeal some through the Justice Sector Reform Project. Bah concludes that real change toward ending violence against women requires a coordinated and sustained effort at many levels, focusing on legal and institutional reforms, with particular attention paid to the repeal of all discriminatory laws and amending ones contradictory to the spirit of the TRC. The development of legislation and ratification of international instruments on gender-based violence is also not enough and so a shift is required that moves from the NGOs' generic awareness programmes on human rights and women's rights to more strategic programmes that address policy issues and operationalising the frameworks that have been developed.

Helen Scanlon and Benilde Nhalevilo maintain this thread in Chapter 6, flagging the structural continuities in a context that is perceived as a success story for localised approaches for transforming conflict. In a rich ethnographic piece that draws on the narratives of a selection of women in Mozambique, the authors point to the widespread violence against women that continues at alarming rates, highlighting the powerful legacy of the conflict for gender relations. Through interviews with a cross-section of Mozambican women this chapter analyses perceptions over the need to address residual gender justice issues. Although there is little available information on the extent of the impact of the conflict in Mozambique on women, it is clear that women and children were the primary victims. In the absence of formal justice mechanisms, women who were abducted or abused during the conflict continue to face social resettlement problems as well as being highly vulnerable to domestic violence. The nation or state political trajectory that Scanlon and Nhalevilo map points to a history where either women were starkly absent or where they did participate, did so on terms mapped by the movements and political organisations of which they were a part. As such the continued absence of gendered considerations in the peace agreement that led to the creation of an independent Mozambican state or the subsequent disarmament, demobilisation and reintegration processes are indicators of a continuing trend of structural inequalities. For instance:

> [A] married woman's resettlement did not solely depend on her family and community, but also on her husband's family. Muianga notes that in Mandlakazi in the southern zone, when women returned, they would go to their own relatives' houses. The family members of married women were responsible for informing their husband's family. If the husband's family were prepared to accept her, the woman was returned to her husband's home.

The authors do not dismiss the presence of normative principles in terms of legislation on land, domestic violence and significant representation of women in parliament. However, a history of entrenched impunity hampers, in the authors' views, the possibilities for real gender equality.

Part 3, the last part of this book, looks at the overall regional context in which security governance is being translated into a normative framework, with a set of agreed standards to which states may commit. This context is important in an era in which regional organisations are increasingly seeking to be relevant to citizens. Two regional institutions are examined in this regard: the African Union and the Economic Community of West African States (ECOWAS).

It is argued that much more than the African Union, the ECOWAS security architecture has made several advances in instituting mechanisms that address the structural roots of conflict. Eka Ikpe's chapter (Chapter 7) provides an opportunity to examine the context and 'ingredients' that have been central to pushing substantive change. ECOWAS has been lauded as exemplary in its institutional engagement with the violent conflicts that beset the West African region through the 1990s and to a lesser extent through the first decade of the 21st century. Its approach has centred on a needs-based process that came into existence as result of a succession of violent conflicts in the sub-region. Its engagement with women in developing a peace and security system has followed an equally long trajectory. This included, among other things, the expansion of the notion of security from a focus on the state to engagement with citizens, which benefited from the key involvement by women activists.

Ikpe notes that the peace and security architecture of ECOWAS clearly reflects a recognition of the gendered experiences of conflict, particularly in one of its most influential instruments to date, the Protocol Relating to the Mechanism for Conflict Prevention, Resolution, Peacekeeping and Security (also known as 'the mechanism'). She goes on to speak to the evolutionary nature of the ECOWAS peace and security architecture, which can be seen in the 2008 development of the ECOWAS Conflict Prevention Framework (ECPF) in which the women, peace and security component recognises 'the promotion of the protection of women through their strategic participation in peace and security processes'. While it is a significant addition to the ECOWAS peace and security architecture, Ikpe cites the conspicuous absence of women in discussions within what may be termed the 'hard security' components, including security governance, practical disarmament and the ECOWAS Standby Force. The spirit of the document is therefore not in practice adequately followed through in its provisions.

Speaking to the conundrum Okech and Alaga both highlight in this book, Ikpe notes that women's participation within these components is tied to a particular narrative which represents women as 'soft', victims, helpful, peacemaking and peace loving. This is especially evident when women feature within the ECPF as mediators, as sources of information, as victims, and as a focus of human rights issues and cross-border initiatives. The bureaucratic challenges of needing to create the space for women's issues to be paid attention to by creating an office and dedicated commissioner to address some of these issues, but at the same time existing parallel structures that focus primarily on 'security' are some of the challenges that continue to plague ECOWAS. The absence of conversations, both in terms of personnel (the numbers of women in senior positions) and programmatically across critical structures that address peace and security, is of concern. The evolutionary nature of ECOWAS, according to Ikpe, indicates the possibilities for change and remedying these glaring oversights. She concludes by recognising the ECPF action plan as an avenue for change.

As the overarching regional body, the African Union with its post-conflict reconstruction and development policy has also articulated a security sector reform policy framework, in addition to naming 2010 the Year of Peace and Security. Chapter 8 by Tim Murithi analyses the extent to which the African Union systematically situates women in the operationalisation of aspects of its peace and security architecture. As a union, Murithi notes, the normative principles are not the challenge, whether these are present in the form of the gender policy, post-conflict reconstruction and development policy or the various offices created to address specific issues of concern to this book such as the Peace and Security Council and the Gender Directorate. What is evident is that despite the pronouncements in the AU's gender policy, the Post-conflict Reconstruction and Development Policy Framework, and in turn the structures under whose purview security falls, are not explicit on gender mainstreaming in peace-building situations. He argues that the AU's gender mainstreaming initiatives in its security governance process have been largely top–down and there is a need for it to do more to actualise its normative claims.

> The [Peace and Security Council] rarely makes reference to ensuring gender equity and promoting gendered decisions on the crisis situations that it assesses. For example, its regular pronouncements on situations in Darfur, Somalia, or the Comoros do not make any explicit references to how the conflict situations are affecting men and women on the ground. The council does not make any reference to the gendered roles of its peacekeepers in the African Union mission in Somalia (AMISOM) and the AU/UN Joint Hybrid Operation in Darfur (UNAMID), nor to how a gender lens should inform the work of the missions.

Nonetheless, Murithi sees an opportunity in the declaration of 2010 as the Year of Peace and Security in Africa. The declaration, he notes, is in part designed to encourage African governments and societies to rethink peace and security paradigms. A re-conceptualisation of how gender mainstreaming can be advanced along the lines developed by feminist scholarship, in particular through the strategic deployment of the concerns generated by gender-based violence, among other challenges, can advance policy debates on how security governance systems can be operationalised and embedded in principles of equity.

Finally, Awino Okech's conclusion draws out the key insights of the book and considers prospects for the future. This volume offers several critical contributions that distinguish it from the growing literature on security governance and gender within that consideration. First, as previously noted, this book benefits from the insights of African scholars and practitioners. Second, the ways in which these processes have developed and context-specific debates in Africa are emphasised in all of the chapters. While this volume does not in any way purport to offer all of the answers, it definitely creates the space within which to re-imagine security governance in a context where so-called empirical data shows that the old ways do not work even when they attempt to take into account the gendered experiences of armed conflict. The importance of an assessment of women's role in unstable contexts such as those that offer the opportunity to re-examine security governance is to offer a useful lens through which we examine critical gains but also major structural continuities that do not offer opportunities for transformation. Given these unique features, we trust that this volume will be of use to both African policymakers and scholars and will provide insights for those working globally on these complex issues.

Reference

Hamber, B., Hillyard, P., Maguire, A., McWilliams, M., Robinson, G., Russell, D. and Ward, M. (2006) 'Discourses in transition: re-imagining women's security', *International Relations*, vol. 20, no. 4, pp. 487–502

Part 1
Conceptual approaches

Evolving narratives of security governance in Africa

'Funmi Olonisakin

Introduction

When closely examined, the notion of security, the roles that security institutions were designed to play, and the governance of those institutions since African states became independent dominions reveal deep structural flaws. Security in Africa was not conceived as a 'common good' for the collective benefit of African peoples. It was created for the benefit of a chosen few – the ruling elite of any given period – for their preservation, and for the control of available resources and the population in the pursuit of this objective. Indeed, two distinct spheres have been apparent throughout African security discourse – that dominated by the elite and that to which ordinary people retreat. This has been sustained with the support of the international community through action or inaction.

Below the radar of states already captured by the ruling elite, ordinary men and women have, over time, devised their own economic, security and justice systems in response to their own needs – mostly, but not all informal and unrecorded. In many cases, private, as well as traditional, customary institutions have stepped into the security and justice gaps created by the absence of the state in the spaces occupied by masses of the population. These systems are not without their own frailties including arbitrariness and exclusionary practices, which invariably leave out the needs and aspirations of certain groups. Not surprisingly, women fall through the cracks in both the elite-driven state systems and the informal non-state arrangements. While women have suffered injustices in state and non-state dominated systems alike, it is not always obvious that demands for women's security and justice must be directed at both.

These state and non-state systems and the conditions that they create have not remained stagnant and completely separate over time. Rather, they have transmutated and responded to critical moments whether in Africa's political development or in the international system. Key moments that have shaped African security discourse have provided important opportunities for a fundamental shift in the discourse. The roles played, for example, by the end of colonial rule, the cold war and its subsequent demise are crucial indicators of shifts in the African security discourse.

This chapter discusses five periods of shifting narratives of African security and the place of the security establishment in the governance of African states. It examines the dominant narratives and actors in Africa's current security environment and asks whether any fundamental change has occurred in who and what defines security, for whom security is provided and how security is governed. The chapter does not focus on the technicalities of how the security establishment is governed. Rather, it concerns itself with one foundational issue: whether the very basis on which security was defined and provided at the creation of the African state has changed, if at all. It argues that evidence of such fundamental change can be found in: whether and how new African voices, not least women's, influence the security discourse; how much external control over the security discourse exists; whether or not there is an emerging convergence between the security narratives of state actors and peoples; and in the processes and rules that inform security provision and governance.

The immediate post-colonial era

On the surface, the African states that became independent dominions in the 1960s mirrored the classical states of the modern state system to which they were birthed. As the 'inheritance elite' – those who took the reigns of power from the colonial rulers – eagerly prepared to take their newly independent states into the United Nations, these new states were accorded, in principle, equal status in the community of states. There was an implicit assumption that the same principles that guided the formation of the modern state also applied to African states. The notion of a 'compact', in which people submitted their sovereignty and paid taxes to the state in return for protection under an agreed political order, was assumed to apply. Thus, presumably, the state would have a monopoly over the means of violence and citizens would periodically choose their leaders and the terms under which they would be governed as part of a seamless process of state reproduction.

The dominant narrative was one of popular sovereignty and this was an attractive proposition to peoples emerging from about a century of foreign domination. The concept of civilian control mirrored the western model handed down at independence (Lee 1969). Observers enthusiastically assumed that these inherited systems would produce strong legitimate civilian institutions, maintaining democratic control over a professional military and security establishment, which would in turn accept a subordinated role to an elected civilian elite (Finer 1988). These assumptions would turn out to be deeply faulty.

In reality, African security in the early post-independence years was the product of a colonial legacy, as was the model of governance Africans inherited. The security and governance arrangements transferred had individual differences depending on the colonising state, but they shared similar functions and legacies for African peoples. In colonial times, the core function of the security establishment was the subjugation of the people to achieve the economic interests of the empire. The inheritance elite retained much of the same structure of governance. The military, police and other parts of the security establishment were part of the transfer of power to African elites (First 1966). Essentially, these structures consolidated a similar security agenda to the previous era – of population and resource control for the protection of the ruling class. The only difference from the colonial regime was the focus on who and what was to be protected. The African elite replaced the colonial rulers as the locus for this protection.

An opportunity for transformation was missed. The military and security establishments were externally imposed without room for national conversations between the inheritance elite and African peoples about the terms on which they would live together and about their collective vision of security. Africa's new ruling elite failed to transform the system for the benefit of the people. In the event, many of the same laws that guided the functioning of the security establishment were retained and they formed the basis of governance in the new states. The people were invariably distanced from main governance processes, not least the governance of the security establishment. The fate of African peoples was effectively sealed at this time. As indicated below, the next few decades would simply entail a process of consolidation of power by the ruling elite – both civilian and military – as one independent state after another fell under dictatorial rule.

By the 1970s, the initial optimism that strong legitimate civilian institutions would emerge in Africa gave way to another wave of developments. Military coups had become the order of the day, with military governments supplanting the earlier civilian regimes in many parts of Africa. Where the coup culture did not take hold, civilian authoritarian regimes had entrenched themselves, with the support of the military. A new narrative emerged among mostly western academics, which proclaimed the military as a modernising force. Military professionalism was seen as a recipe for effective military intervention in politics (Janowitz 1977) with no sound justification.

African states were in essence captured by authoritarian and dictatorial regimes in part because the cold war system enabled it. The bipolar division of the international system into two blocs (East and West), exemplified by the ideological divide and a nuclear arms race between two superpowers, the US and the former Soviet Union, had a profound effect on Africa. The restraining danger of superpower nuclear confrontation kept war off European soil for four and a half decades from the end of the Second World War in 1945 until the outbreak of the war in former Yugoslavia in 1991. But for much of that period, Africa and other parts of the developing world became the theatre for superpower competition. Each bloc provided support (often in the form of military and economic aid) to client states on the basis of their ideological leanings. In that cold war environment, in which ideology mattered more than the internal order of states, Africa's ruling elite succeeded in entrenching themselves in power with foreign support.

A third shift occurred which revised the argument that the military was a modernising force. Rather, the military and security establishment was considered to be less of a modernising force (Decalo 1976) given further evidence that in many cases the military elite was equally incapable of forging national unity. A small elite presided over fragmented institutions, which lacked the capacity to effectively govern security establishments with a national character (Luckham 1971; see Hutchful and Bathily 1998). In reality, African armed forces were nothing like the cohesive structures expected to emerge from the models transferred from the West. Whether in government or in support of a group of the civilian elite, the security establishment became a tool for the repression of legitimate opposition, at times through severe force. This method of securing the regime also implied that much-needed resources would be diverted from productive sectors to support of regime security.

Despite all of this, it was difficult to sustain these structures. The state and security establishment could not function in isolation from the larger society on which they were superimposed. After all, that larger society consisted of various traditional structures, among other systems, which predated colonial rule (see Foucault 1980). The over-reliance on ruling by the use of force was simply not adequate. Invariably, many of these authoritarian systems would face collapse because of their failure to respond to the overall security needs of the environment. This was a key factor in the subsequent collapse of authoritarian regimes.

A fourth shift in narrative occurred at the end of the cold war from around 1990. This was the first time that space opened up for dialogue, even if a violent one, between state actors and those previously excluded. The end of bipolar, superpower rivalry meant that the old conditions for great power support to client states in Africa were no longer applicable. Indeed, the conditionality for aid to African states changed. Democracy and good governance replaced ideology as the new basis for foreign assistance to African states. This removed the lid from seemingly latent internal conflicts underpinned by grievances among excluded groups. Up until then, the most prominent voices on African security had been those of the state and of western analysts. Security was not an accessible subject matter in which ordinary people could engage. New actors emerged with new narratives that emphasised security concerns beyond the state-centric ones of the previous decades. The absence of state protection for masses of citizens both in the private sphere and in public settings became the dominant narrative that leaders could not ignore.

The rising opposition to the state could no longer be curtailed as non-state groups increasingly contested control of state power. By 1990, when the cold war was generally considered over, only five sub-Saharan African states could be considered to have had a semblance of democratic rule. It was inevitable that change would be demanded by populations that were long excluded from power without redress, as was the case in many African countries. Regime change occurred peacefully and piecemeal in some countries (e.g. Benin, Malawi, Mali). In others, the demand for change led to violent conflict as seen in Liberia and Sierra Leone. As armed conflict spread across the continent (Somalia, Congo, Rwanda, etc) concerns about the absence of state protection for ordinary people became real. The armed conflicts that were unleashed in Africa were some of the most brutal and the innocent were not spared as civilian casualties rose to an unprecedented level. Indeed, as Awino Okech points out in Chapter 3, it was these brutal conflicts and their consequences for civilian populations, not least the gendered dimensions of those conflicts, which drew global attention to the plight of women and constructed powerful new narratives about women not just as victims but as agents of change.

In any event, the expected change did not occur. These conflicts did not produce national conversations between African leaders and their peoples. Instead, aggrieved elites hijacked the grievances and narratives of ordinary people, preventing the development of a genuine peoples' movement. Indeed, none of the brutal armed conflicts which broke out at the end of the cold war (Liberia, Sierra Leone, Côte d'Ivoire, DRC, among others) was the product of a people-led movement for change. Rather, they were intense struggles between elite groupings. In the end, civilians who should have formed the locus of support for a movement for change became the focus of the violence in these conflicts. That Africa is yet to have a people-led process of change and of genuine state reproduction is evident as the new ruling elites are yet to

21

fully recognise or indeed accept the centrality of the people in the process of governance.

The fifth and latest shift in the narrative concerns the process of building peace in the various conflict-affected states and addressing the fracture that has eventually become apparent even within states that did not experience large-scale armed conflict. For the first time, there is a return to the discourse about the control of the security establishment by elected civilians. What is more significant is that security is seen in a broader context to include not just the defence and protection of citizens, but also economic and social justice. Security is being redefined beyond the narrow lens of state actors and this discourse has hints of transformation.

Whose narrative has been dominant up until this period? The voices of those excluded from earlier narratives only came to the fore towards the end of this latest era. For the first time, women have become an increasingly visible part of the African security dialogue in what remains a largely male-dominated environment. Accounts of the insecurity experienced by women in times of peace and war and the need for women to exercise their agency in the formal realm have made it to the fore of international attention. The security establishment, in whichever way it has been defined over time, has been male dominated. Women have been involved in the security establishment only to the extent that they serve the needs of men as wives, sex workers and auxiliary workers (Enloe 1988). Similarly, authoritarian and military regimes across much of Africa excluded women from key power or decision-making positions. Where women had a history of participation in armed conflict, they failed in large part to consolidate in peacetime the gains made during war, with few exceptions. They were and are simply relegated to gendered roles and excluded from command positions and decision-making positions – whether in the security establishment or political life.

Redirecting the state's vision of security remains a major challenge. How can reconstruction efforts ensure that security is provided as a 'public good'? For the first time since the immediate post-independent years, another opportunity is presented which might allow for exploration of a genuine social contract. Might it be possible for the people to submit their sovereignty in exchange for the kind of protection which might better guarantee state reproduction? The African security narrative has clearly shifted to one which emphasises inclusive peace building and the building of states capable of responding to the security needs of their citizens collectively, rather than guaranteeing the security of a select few. It is on this current shift and the extent to which it becomes grounded in reality that the rest of this chapter will now focus.

Security reform in peace and state building

Various actors and competing narratives have emerged in the effort to build peace and states capable of and willing to be more responsive to citizens' needs. The narratives of the different actors, including state institutions, international bodies and the supposed recipients of security including women, youth and communities, are not quite converging. As earlier indicated, the changes that occurred at the end of the cold war have produced a new international agenda for African security. From the 1990s, an attempt to redefine security beyond the exclusive focus on the state gained ground globally.

In a new dispensation in which the dialogues about state (re) building have dominated the discourse, a fundamental shift in the conception of security has occurred: a case has been made for an African security agenda that encompasses individual and collective security, whereby internal and external security are seen as two sides of the same coin (Ball and Fayemi 2004). Recognition of the need to shift from state- and elite-focused security to a security that places individuals at its centre, widely referred to as human security, has gained ground across the global South, although, as discussed later in this chapter, the extent to which this is applied in practice is questionable.

While African analysts and academics have been at the centre of this conceptual debate, the policy and practical engagement has been influenced almost entirely by the international donor community. Donor narratives of security reform and the process of change that ought to prevail in Africa have dominated efforts to reform security governance in Africa. This applies to a broad range of efforts, whether undertaken by the ruling elite or by international organisations – most especially the United Nations – through peacekeeping operations or coalitions of other actors (such as the British Military Advisory and Training Team in Sierra Leone), and in exceptional cases, private security actors (as seen in Liberia). Donor narratives and approaches have had a significant influence on how security sector reform programmes are undertaken in Africa. Those narratives and approaches are not entirely consistent with the reality on the ground, some of the reasons for which are discussed below.

External narratives are dominated by the assumption that state security actors ought to form the sole focus of reform. This is a return to the model superimposed on African states at independence, which presupposed state monopoly of the means of violence and in particular, the existence or the potential to create strong civilian institutions able to maintain control of the security establishment. Indeed, while recognising that in their broken state many African states do not have this capacity, there is a tendency for external actors to assume that the recreation of precisely this capacity is what is required. Thus it is usual to find so-called security sector reform programmes focused on the professionalisation of the military through training of the military, the police and related services and sometimes training for parliamentarians on civilian oversight.

However, external support in this way takes little cognisance of the reality on the ground. The structural basis for the kind of reform being focused on is mostly flawed. In many situations, the legal and constitutional framework underpinning these reforms remain the same. In countries like Nigeria, Ghana and Zambia, for example, the police acts of the colonial era have remained in force. Training security personnel without a transformation of the legal and policy framework that governs them amounts to no more than a cosmetic attempt at reform. Moreover, the average African state does not have a monopoly over the means of violence. A plethora of other security actors are often in existence, offering protection as private commercial actors or as informal security providers in various communities. They have their own decision-making and governance processes. International and state actors ignore them at the peril of the various security reform initiatives that they champion. Focusing reform efforts solely on the formal institutions of the state reinforces the status quo and continues to exclude the masses of people who rely on informal actors and systems to respond to their needs.

The narratives of African peoples, particularly women, are not consistent with the approaches of the donor and international community-led security sector reform processes witnessed in the last decade as part of the remaking of African states. Two factors are worthy of note about these narratives. First, the security and justice of the poor and marginalised are not among the priority security concerns of states. Therefore, state security institutions in much of Africa still do not respond to the security needs of the vast majority of populations. Rather, as indicated above, other non-state, informal security actors respond to the security needs of the poor and marginalised (Olonisakin, Ikpe and Badong 2009). Second, women's security and justice concerns are not high on the agenda of either state or non-state security actors. Indeed, the treatment of women's security concerns in existing security arrangements, whether in the formal or informal realm, is perhaps the most glaring indicator of whether or not the governance of security in a given context has been transformed.

The narratives of the poor and the marginalised in Africa about the nature of their security and justice needs and the sources of provision of those needs are invariably mostly at odds with the state or regime's pattern of provision of justice and security. In the broadest sense, security in much of Africa is about protection against local crime and of personal security, protection of land, property and livestock, access to justice – such as raising bail or paying fines – and the resolution of community disputes (DFID 2004). Interestingly, however, these groups tend to gravitate toward the informal systems of security and justice and rely less on state security and justice systems, which in theory are supposed to protect all citizens.

There is a range of explanations for this continued failure of African elites, whether in post-war situations or other transforming states, to pay attention to the security needs of ordinary people. One is of particular relevance to the present discussion. This is the fact that the peace settlements that resulted from the different post-cold war conflicts and the transitions that are taking place across the region are the product of elite bargains and not the result of a genuine compact between the ruling elite and the people. As indicated earlier in this chapter, the violent conflicts that occurred at the end of the cold war were not a people's war, but an appropriation of the people's legitimate grievances by an aggrieved elite in pursuit of intra-elite conflict. As a result, the current post-conflict, post-settlement security arrangements are still skewed in favour of the elite and not the people.

Yet, even the informal systems to which ordinary women and men retreat are also afflicted by similar problems of exclusion and power imbalances, which further marginalise some already excluded groups. There is diversity even among the excluded who seek protection from the informal systems, such that the security concerns of certain groups are invariably left out. This is the case with women, for whom, like all other citizens, security is also about protection against crime and violence – a different kind of violence, which is not necessarily viewed as a crime by the community and by the very people on whom they depend for protection. Issues such as domestic violence, rape, incest and female genital mutilation rarely make it to the agenda of non-state security and justice systems. Similarly, protection of land and property is not achievable for women in places where they are not allowed to own or inherit property. Access to justice is much harder if women are not recognised by the law or if informal work is not remunerated and so they are unable to meet the costs of seeking justice in the courts (Olonisakin, Ikpe and Badong 2009). Women who are caught up in these situations become doubly invisible to state and non-state institutions.

The situation of women

Women's security concerns are invariably caught in a void between the formal and the informal worlds of security governance. That security provision for women has hardly changed over the last five decades reveals the true state of security governance in Africa. On the surface, actors have changed and spaces have been expanded for the inclusion of new actors, but in reality, the interests and frameworks that sustain the status quo remain entrenched. Some of these include legal and constitutional frameworks which dictate the terms on which security is to be provided and governed. It remains the case that the management and oversight of the formal security establishment has been the preserve of the elite groupings in government, which rarely included elected representatives of the people. Contested election outcomes further diminish the legitimacy of those supposedly responsible for security oversight. Similar frameworks, such as customary laws and practices, prevail in informal systems, some of which discriminate against women. Without a fundamental reordering of these frameworks, reform initiatives cannot achieve the desired transformation in security governance.

How can such frameworks be altered to take into account the concerns of women and other excluded groups? Without political will on the part of the ruling elite, it is virtually impossible to alter existing legal and constitutional frameworks notwithstanding the determination of other critical actors. But apart from national frameworks, international norms have also evolved, in part to improve the status of women and provide legitimacy to a range of actors at regional and national levels (e.g. regional organisations and civil society actors). Of particular relevance in this regard is the adoption of United Nations Security Council Resolution 1325 (UNSC Resolution 1325) on women, peace and security.

UNSC Resolution 1325 calls on member states to ensure that gender is mainstreamed throughout all conflict-prevention and peace-building initiatives, not least within UN peace missions. It also affirms women's rights to be involved in decision making on peace and security issues and to take on leadership positions in these areas. It is tempting to see the issue of women's participation in decision making purely in terms of numbers. But as indicated by Okech in Chapter 3, there are structural factors that lie at the heart of the challenge. Merely increasing the numbers of women in security institutions, for example, will not transform the norms and culture of those institutions. This resolution is nonetheless an important normative instrument for pursuing women's security agenda.

An assessment of the impact of UNSC Resolution 1325 across a number of national and regional contexts is the focus of other studies (see Olonisakin, Barnes and Ikpe 2010). While it is difficult to render precise judgement or to accurately measure its impact, investigation across these contexts suggest that UNSC Resolution 1325 has had marginal impact in Africa and other places. The reasons for this are not far fetched. The same structural flaws that have shaped security governance in Africa invariably limit the application of the resolution in target countries. Nonetheless, there is some evidence, even if anecdotal, that over time, a mutually reinforcing process in which international and regional actors and civil society push for change can ultimately make national and other actors alter their stance. That UNSC Resolution 1325 is itself the product of civil society advocacy, with the support of several UN member states, makes this point (see Olonisakin, Barnes and Ikpe 2010).

Already, the evolution of new norms within continental and regional organisations (such as the AU and ECOWAS, discussed respectively by Tim Murithi in Chapter 8 and Eka Ikpe in Chapter 7) serves to complement UNSC Resolution 1325, which finds opportunities for implementation in conflict and post-conflict settings. Beyond conflict-affected contexts, Africa is experiencing other transitions, not least those from long-term authoritarian rule. These contexts lend themselves to change in varying degrees. UNSC Resolution 1325 and similar international and regional instruments discussed in this book provide an appropriate framework for normative change that can in turn improve the lot of women.

What, if anything, has changed?

This assessment of the shifts in African security narratives across five decades throws up more of the same questions and few answers. Given the new efforts to redefine security – the inclusion of women's and other excluded voices in this notwithstanding – has the basis for the definition and provision of security changed? Has the purpose for which security establishments were created changed? Are international actors dominating the scene or are Africans taking more control of this discourse?

As indicated in the introductory part of this chapter, the litmus test for inclusive security and for good governance of security is whether or not there is an emerging convergence between the narratives within the security systems (state and non-state) and of African peoples, particularly the traditionally excluded groups. African women and their core concerns remain far removed from the formal and informal systems of security provision and governance. This is the single most important indicator that a fundamental shift has not occurred in African security governance. Though now defined on the basis of the needs of both state and citizens, the role of the ruling elite and state security institutions has hardly changed. Neither the purpose for which security institutions were created nor the rules governing their functioning has undergone any transformation.

Clearly, some historical moments within and outside Africa provided opportunities for structural change. This was the case with the end of colonial rule and the end of the cold war. But in general, these moments were not seized despite the transformational potential in the narratives that developed around them. Excluded groups and those who clamour for improvement in their situations – whether local or international actors – need a reality check. The dominant narratives are invariably those of the power holders at any given moment. Africa's ruling elites remain the beneficiaries of state security systems largely backed by internationally driven policies and initiatives which ignore or miss the reality on the ground, while the parallel informal systems on the margins of the state appropriate the available informal security systems. The emergence of historical moments and new actors alike will no doubt offer opportunities to rewrite the rules. In these changing vicissitudes, old and new narratives will compete for pre-eminence. Ultimately, the extent to which women become included will tell us who, and what system, has won the day.

References

Ball, Nicole and Fayemi, J. Kayode (2004) *A Handbook on Security Sector Governance in Africa*, Nigeria, Centre for Democracy and Development

Decalo, S. (1976) *Coups and Army Rule in Africa: Studies in Military Style*, London, Yale University Press

Department for International Development (DFID) (2004) *Non-State Justice and Security Systems*, DFID Briefing, http://www.gsdrc.org/docs/open/SSAJ101.pdf, accessed 27 May 2010

Enloe, C. (1988) *Does Khaki Become You? The Militarisation of Women's Lives*, London, Pandora Press

Finer, S.E. (1988) *The Man on Horseback: The Role of the Military in Politics*, second edition, London, Pinter

First, Ruth (1966) *The Barrel of a Gun: Political Power in Africa and the Coup d'Etat*, London, Penguin

Foucault, M. (1980) *Power/Knowledge: Selected Interviews and Other Writings 1972–1977*, Hemel Hempstead, Harvester Wheatsheaf

Hutchful, E. and Bathily, A. (eds) (1998) *The Military and Militarism in Africa*, Dakar, CODESRIA

Janowitz, M. (1977) *Military Institutions and Coercion in the Developing Nations*, Chicago, Chicago University Press

Lee, J.M. (1969) *African Armies and Civil Order*, London, Chatto and Windus

Luckham, R. (1971) *The Nigerian Military: A Sociological Analysis of Authority and Revolt*, Cambridge, Cambridge University Press

Olonisakin, F., Barnes, K. and Ikpe, E. (2010) *Women, Peace and Security: Translating Policy into Practice*, London, Routledge

Olonisakin, F., Ikpe, E. and Badong, P. (2009) 'The future of security and justice for the poor', *CSDG Policy Studies*, no. 21, Conflict, Security and Development Group, March

2

Security sector reform: re-imagining its transformative potential

Comfort Ero

Feminist literature has drawn attention to the importance of the post-war moment for transforming unequal power relations and furthering gender justice (Meintjes et al 2001). Similarly, gender advocates within the field of transitional justice refer to opportunities that exist in post-conflict settings to promote 'fundamental women's rights reform' (Scanlon and Muddell 2009: 11). But how real are the opportunities in the transitional contexts for setting a transformative agenda in ways that include a women's agenda? Preventing the recurrence of human rights violations and promoting social reconstruction as well as the rule of law are key objectives of transitional justice. In pursuing these objectives, what spaces are created and what gains have emerged to bring to the fore a gendered perspective that impacts on post-conflict governance in general and, specifically, on security governance, a core theme of this book? Does transitional justice provide a foundation for women to advance policies that transform patriarchal gender relations and situate women's concerns within a new post-repressive or post-conflict governance arrangement?

In answering these questions, I begin this chapter with a discussion of transitional justice approaches, looking at core goals and objectives that could create space for women's agendas in transitional contexts and locate women's rights at the centre of post-conflict reconstruction and transformation (the first two sections). As the theme of this book is the potential for locating women's agendas within security governance discourse on the

African continent, the third section of this chapter will focus specifically on whether security sector reform, as understood by transitional justice practitioners, can provide a gendered perspective that challenges the existing patriarchal structures and assumptions on which Africa's security sector is grounded. Using the notion of 're-imagining security', as conceived by Hamber et al (2006), I argue that there are real possibilities for engendering security governance in policy and practice if decision makers engage with the insecurities that confront women. There are real concerns, however, about the limits of institutional (and security sector) reform in influencing the lives of ordinary citizens in transitional contexts. Limitations in both the design and implementation of security sector governance programmes, as well as the ad hoc approach to engendering the security sector, undercut its potential to contribute to a transformative security agenda that is inclusive of women's needs.

It is against this background that the final section of the chapter concludes on a less than optimistic note on the possibilities for situating women's security concerns within new security governance arrangements. While the transitional moment does create opportunities for change to emerge, these are often fleeting; there are few (if any) examples where gains were successfully consolidated, or resulted in a transformed society with gender equality. Further, transitional justice is also slow to broaden its scope to ensure its relevance to other transitional processes, such as constitutional reform or transformation to ensure a more just society. This limits its potential to contribute to real transformation in ways that include gender issues in security governance (and governance in general) in transitional contexts.

Transitional justice and post-conflict transformation

Transitional justice refers to a range of approaches undertaken by societies to respond to systematic and widespread violations of human rights. It provides societies seeking to address the wrongdoing of previous regimes with a variety of judicial and non-judicial responses, including criminal prosecution, truth-seeking, institutional reform (including vetting and dismissal) and reparations programmes (including state-sponsored memorialisation efforts). This list is not exhaustive as many societies have developed other creative approaches to deal with past abuses, such as the use of local or community-based (sometimes referred to as traditional or indigenous-based) approaches to addressing human rights violations.

Central to transitional justice are several interrelated or overlapping goals. These include the importance of attempting to heal divisions in society that arise as a result of human rights violations; bringing closure to and healing the wounds of individuals, groups and/or society as a whole; providing justice to victims and ensuring accountability for perpetrators; creating an accurate historical record for society; restoring the rule of law and reforming institutions that promote the rule of law and human rights; ensuring that human rights violations are not repeated; and promoting lasting peace. In another form, transitional justice has two normative goals: redress and justice for victims (which places obligations on states to recognise, acknowledge and provide relief) and the creation of a new, just political order that promotes peace, reconciliation and democracy (Arthur 2009a: 357).

Transitional justice advocates point to the 'limited reach' of each approach to deliver the desired justice or transformation (see Arthur 2009b: 16; de Grieff 2010: 5) in highly complex transitional settings of the kind witnessed on the continent. Adding to the problem are multiple issues that relate to the very founding of the state. It is for this reason that advocates in this field emphasise the need to adopt a holistic strategy to transitional justice because no single mechanism is capable of sufficiently addressing the huge demand for justice. As Arthur notes:

> a holistic approach to [transitional justice] is of vital importance – not in achieving the desired transformation, which is too high a goal for [transitional justice], but rather in empowering key actors who may make such transformation possible. A range of initiatives will be necessary, not just judicial and non-judicial forms of accountability, but also reform of state and important social institutions. (Arthur 2009b: 16)

Thus, a holistic strategy would entail reparations, whether material or symbolic. These are most effective when paired with the needs identified by victims in truth commission processes. Truth commissions can be a critical first step in the search for justice; they can ensure that documentary evidence is preserved for future prosecutions. Prosecutions are, however, unlikely to succeed in ending impunity unless accompanied by serious efforts at institutional reform.

Transitional justice advocates also note that no country in transition can claim to have successfully pursued a comprehensive set of transitional justice measures (de Grieff 2010: 5). This point demonstrates that context matters: how various measures evolve and take shape depends largely on the transitional context and on the impact of political agreements between elites, including perpetrators (i.e. elite pacting). Other competing societal agendas will also have an impact on the transformative potential of transitional justice measures (a point that I will return to in my conclusion). It is also worth noting that post-war reconstruction can happen in spite of, or in the absence of, transitional justice measures. One can cite the example of South Africa, where the constitution-making process, and other steps to dismantle apartheid, had a far greater transformative effect on the lives of ordinary people than the Truth and Reconciliation Commission (TRC) process. One can also refer to Mozambique, where 'peace' was attained in the absence of transitional justice measures (see Chapter 6).

Transitional justice for women?

It is widely recognised that in most contemporary conflicts women and children are especially vulnerable to human rights violations. Women are frequently subjected to violence in ways specific to their gender. Sexual violence, for example, has been integral to war strategies in many conflict situations, on the African continent and elsewhere. Sierra Leone's Truth and Reconciliation Commission estimates that as many as 70 per cent of women were victims of gender-based violence during that country's 11-year conflict (SLTRC 2004). During armed conflicts, pre-existing inequalities and patterns of discrimination that women face on a day-to-day basis (as a result of their marginalisation and poverty) are often exacerbated.

Women are also at risk of double victimisation: they are discriminated against as women, but are just as likely as men to be victims in conflict situations. While women are killed or abducted or suffer direct physical violence,[1] they are also victims of gender-specific violations such as sexual violence. As mothers and wives of those who have disappeared, been tortured or killed, they are also secondary victims. Women are also harmed in other ways in the aftermath of conflict. These include long-term bodily harm and damage to their health as a result of the curtailment of reproductive freedom, the loss of land, insecurity, an increased burden of care, political exclusion, economic hardship and vulnerability.

Not all women experience conflict in the same way. Indeed, many perform a variety of roles in conflict situations, including as combatants should they decide to take up arms. Some engage in peace work in the non-governmental sector; others participate in the peace process; in many instances, women become heads of households. The reversal of traditional roles, such as through the growth of female-headed households, forces women to sustain their families in ways that may be outside their experience. Many women have to develop a variety of coping or survival strategies, one of which is to play a greater role in the informal sector. A gendered perspective of transitional justice must recognise the various gender violations that exist and the multiple roles that women may have to adopt (Meintjes et al 2001: 5–8; Scanlon and Muddell 2009).

Until recently, the experience of women in political violence and civil war was often overlooked by transitional justice initiatives, largely as a result of gender-blind definitions of human rights violations. Today, there is greater awareness among transitional justice practitioners of the need to broaden the field to better address women's experience in conflict and to challenge pre-existing gender inequalities that lead to discrimination against women. At the same time, as noted above, gender justice advocates point to opportunities 'to promote women's leadership, enhance access to justice, and build momentum for fundamental women's rights reform' in the aftermath of conflicts (Scanlon and Muddell 2009: 11). While women and their organisations are seriously under-represented during peace negotiations, 'transitional justice mechanisms offer women other opportunities to participate in and influence the peace-building process' (Scanlon and Muddell 2009: 11). The question remains, however, whether these opportunities result in the inclusion of women's concerns in transitional processes, and whether this in fact yields tangible results that have an impact on the lives of women. There is great concern about the unevenness and inconsistency of the inclusion of gender considerations in the design and implementation of transitional justice measures (Scanlon and Muddell 2009: 10).

Analysis of previous transitional justice processes emerged in the 1980s and early 1990s as a result of truth commission mandates, judicial opinions, and policy proposals for reparations. These attempts at analysis have usually been 'written, interpreted, and implemented with little regard for the distinct and complex gender-based violations' suffered by women (Scanlon and Muddell 2009: 11). Neglect of gendered patterns of abuse affects the access of both men and women to justice in a variety of ways: by limiting the reach of reparations programmes; entrenching impunity; distorting the historical record; and undermining the legitimacy of transitional justice initiatives. Moreover, there is still very little understanding of the gendered legacies of authoritarianism, of the complex and shifting relationship between different types of violence, and of the challenges and opportunities present in transitional contexts to enhance gender justice (ICTJ 2008a).

There has been notable progress towards rectifying these shortcomings in recent transitional justice processes. In Africa's post-conflict environments, as in other settings, gender concerns have become increasingly tied to other transitional justice processes that seek redress for crimes committed during periods of violent repression or war and offer holistic perspectives to prevent the recurrence. For example, the development of new jurisprudence in international law since the mid-1990s has provided more targeted ways of responding to gender-based violations. Landmark cases heard in the international criminal tribunals for the former Yugoslavia and Rwanda saw rape being defined as a crime against humanity.

The pervasive nature of gender-based violence against women gained further international recognition when, in 1998, the Rome Statute, which created the International Criminal Court (ICC), recognised rape, sexual slavery, enforced prostitution, forced pregnancy, enforced sterilisation, or any other form of sexual violence of comparable gravity as crimes against humanity and war crimes.[2] Similarly, the creation of the Special Court for Sierra Leone (SCSL) in 2000 resulted in several ground-breaking legal developments that have had a significant impact on the field of international gender justice (Scanlon and Muddell 2009: 15). Along with the ICC, the SCSL recognised gender crimes in its definition of crimes against humanity and widened its interpretation of this crime to include sexual slavery and forced marriage (Scanlon and Muddell 2009: 15).

Other transitional justice approaches, such as truth commissions, have made significant advances in enhancing women's rights through the holding of thematic gender hearings. The mandates of the Sierra Leone and Liberian truth commissions called for special attention to be paid to issues of gender justice. In addition, truth commissions, such as that in Sierra Leone, have increasingly documented patterns of gender-based violence and investigated the root causes of conflict. Emanating from these findings of truth commissions are recommendations that speak about the need to develop new legislation that contributes to changing the lives of women or to the reform of various state institutions, such as those in the security sector. In Sierra Leone, for example, the truth commission used information gathered on gender-based violence to recommend changes to discriminatory laws that made women vulnerable to the violence that occurred during the conflict and to the continuation of such abuse in the post-conflict period.

Similarly, reparations measures have helped to ensure the inclusion of women's issues in post-conflict justice and governance processes. Reparations are the transitional justice measure most directly focused on victims and which offers a 'transformative potential' (Rubio-Marín 2009: 17, 381–402) to enhance the lives of women in post-conflict settings. In many cases, reparations may be the only form of justice victims receive, particularly those women who are often marginalised by formal justice or truth-seeking measures (Muddell 2009). The right of victims to reparations for gross violations of internationally recognised human rights is enshrined in several multilateral treaties and is now also recognised in international law. In a 2005 resolution the

United Nations General Assembly outlined five components of the right to remedy and reparations, namely restitution (returning the victim to their situation before the crime was committed); compensation (payment for economically measurable damage); rehabilitation (more general medical and social assistance); satisfaction (a broad group of measures that includes access to justice and truth-seeking); and guarantees of non-repetition.

Reparations policy can provide greater focus in formulating a gendered approach. In the past, reparations were aimed at addressing specific violations. This reflected a limited view of human rights violations centring on deaths, disappearances and imprisonment. Reparation policies had often failed to recognise the specific abuses suffered by women during periods of conflict, such as rape, sexual slavery and displacement. Following the United Nations' General Assembly adoption of the 'Basic Principles and Guidelines on the Right to a Remedy and Reparation for Victims of Gross Violations of International Human Rights Law and Serious Violations of International Humanitarian Law' (UN 2007), a number of women's organisations mobilised to ensure that reparations policies were more responsive to victims of gender-based violence. This led to the 2007 Nairobi Declaration (UAF-A et al 2007), which redefines reparations and guides policymaking for implementing the rights of victims of sexual violence.

This declaration was a response to the failure of the UN to adequately incorporate gender concerns in its guidelines on the right to reparations. The declaration noted that gender-based violence committed during conflicts 'is the result of inequalities between women and men, girls and boys, that predated the conflict, and … this violence continues to aggravate the discrimination of women and girls in post-conflict situations'. It therefore declared that 'Reparations must go above and beyond the immediate reasons and consequences of the crimes and violations; they must aim to address the political and structural inequalities that negatively shape women's and girls' lives.' The one shortcoming of the declaration is that it focuses on women and neglects the increasingly frequent acts of sexual violence perpetrated against men and boys.

Despite the progressive recommendations contained in the declaration, there are still many challenges to the delivery of a gendered approach to reparations that might also contribute to a more transformative agenda for transitional justice. Two book projects of the International Centre for Transitional Justice (ICTJ) on gender and reparations sought to provide a systematic study of previous experiences; this would enable greater cross-fertilisation of lessons from various contexts and assist the development of a more effective response (Rubio-Marín 2006 and 2009). In analysing the various experiences of reparations, both studies conclude that women's experience of post-conflict reparations is varied. Indeed, a number of themes recur in these books and these are often reiterated by gender activists. They include:

- the weakness of reparations programmes in incorporating women's needs in their design or implementation
- the failure to recognise and address structural issues (i.e. inequalities) which have given rise to gender-based violations of human rights and whose continued existence ensures the preservation of the status quo
- the need to recognise the continuities between crimes committed before, during and after periods of conflict
- the poor implementation of these programmes, largely as a result of a lack of accessible information about these processes, and the inability of women to control their family finances.

The second point is central to our concern: if not properly managed, reparations may reinforce existing structural inequalities. If reparations are to be effective, they should have a transformative agenda and should not return women (or other vulnerable groups) to a situation in which they once again face discrimination and violence. Reparations programmes should provide an opportunity, however modest, for women to rebuild their lives.

Probably the best example of the transformative potential of reparations measure is Morocco. The Moroccan Equity and Reconciliation Commission (Instance Equité et Réconciliation or IER) was the world's first truth commission with the power to grant reparations directly. It was established by royal decree on 7 January 2004 to investigate instances of enforced disappearance and arbitrary detention between 1956 and 1999, to issue reparations to victims, to provide recommendations on other measures for victims, and to establish a reliable historical record of abuses.

There were a number of women in key places, although only one woman served as a commissioner in the 17-member commission (ICTJ 2005). No women were appointed to two of the three working groups of the IER (for investigations, reparations and research), thereby reducing the attention paid to gender issues. Most women appearing before the commission were not victims of direct violence, but were affected nonetheless by the repressive regime of King Hassan II and were in desperate need of social and economic assistance.

Previous reparations benefits had been based on traditional laws of inheritance that prioritised eldest sons over wives, and usually left widows destitute and/or reliant on male relatives for survival.[3] In an effort to avoid replicating these gender hierarchies, the IER proposed that a more equitable share of reparations be given to the spouses of those who had died or disappeared (Muddell 2009). To avoid unilaterally defining the violations committed against the women involved in the transitional justice process, the commission tried to take account of their differing experiences and backgrounds when making recommendations (CCDH 2008).

The Moroccan truth commission influenced changes in the way reparations were awarded to women by focusing on a communal reparations programme which included women from regions that had suffered from collective punishment or isolation (due to the presence of the secret detention centres). The programme represents one of the most advanced exercises in the field of collective reparations. It acknowledged past abuses and preserved their memory by converting former detention compounds into social, cultural and economic centres and memorials (IER 2006).

Re-imagining reform's transformative potential

Of particular relevance to this book, however, is security sector reform and whether this can be achieved through alternative approaches that are not state-centric, and which help shape a security governance discourse that takes account of women's concerns. The reform of the security sector has become part of the transitional justice approach in countries in transition because state security agencies (the army, police, paramilitaries and state-controlled militias, as well as non-state security forces such as rebel groups) 'are often the most serious perpetrators of human rights violations' (Scanlon and Muddell 2009: 21).

A transitional justice approach places justice at the centre of the reform process and requires a more 'justice-sensitive approach' that responds to legacies of massive and serious abuse. Transitional justice advocates maintain that four elements are relevant to the transformation of abusive security systems. These are: building institutional integrity to discourage abuses; promoting the legitimacy of the security sector to overcome the crisis of trust characteristic of situations where there have been serious abuses; empowering all citizens, but especially victims of oppression and violence and other marginalised groups, through their involvement in reform processes; and enhancing coherence with other transitional justice approaches (such as criminal prosecutions, truth-telling and reparations) so as to increase the effectiveness of each of these measures (ICTJ 2008b; Scanlon and Muddell 2009: 21).

A comprehensive transitional justice approach not only identifies individual perpetrators, but also looks closely at the structural deficiencies of governance systems that allow for human rights abuses. Initiatives to re-establish the rule of law and democratic norms in the security apparatus of a country would therefore include both non-criminal forms of accountability (vetting and lustration programmes) and the more general re-establishment of the rule of law. Vetting and lustration programmes provide one way of purging the security sector of officials responsible for crimes, or who are simply guilty of association with the previous regime.

While these initiatives may help to establish an institutional blank slate for a new government, they often focus exclusively on combatants and neglect victims of violence. They offer little by way of alternative thinking with regard to the reform of the security sector, and in particular with regard to addressing the insecurities that affect women. Gender-related concerns are frequently overlooked or perceived as unimportant in security sector governance (Scanlon and Muddell 2009: 22). The editors of this book have posed the question: what would a women's agenda propose in relation to security sector governance? One way of answering this would be to consider the 're-imagining of security away from institutional and patriarchal approaches towards contextualised, bottom–up approaches' (Hamber et al 2006: 488). This would privilege the perspectives of ordinary people, and in particular women, in the creation of a new security governance structure. Consideration should be given to moving beyond the current practice of achieving institutional reform through gender quotas to re-socialising men and women to develop more 'nuanced and different understandings of security'. Such an approach would also shift the discourse away from traditional interpretations of security (as having to do with perceived threats, territorial security and deterrence (Hamber et al 2006: 491)), to one that provides a broader conceptual framework for understanding and addressing the security concerns of ordinary citizens.

This conceptual broadening is part of a 'gendered security approach', an approach that can be characterised as:

> centralising gender in analyses of what have been termed 'traditional' security concerns – such as violent conflict – and what have been termed 'non-traditional' security concerns – such as health, economic empowerment and political participation. Gendered security empowers women and men to re-imagine security in ways which can then inform bottom–up, contextualised approaches. Gendered security will be of particular utility for women, who often demand mass-scale social transformation during post-conflict transition processes. One key means of achieving such a transformation is through the empowerment of women to re-imagine security. (Hamber et al 2006: 491)

In their study of women's views on security in three transitional settings, Lebanon, Northern Ireland and South Africa, Hamber et al found that post-conflict security involved three interrelated factors. First, security was 're-imagined' to include economic security; this entails independence and freedom from male dominance at home (which itself can lead to physical violence).[4] Second, security has been 're-imagined' to mean combating gender-related violence, not just through the creation of new laws (which can be transformative if implemented), but also by ensuring that such crimes are seen as abhorrent acts; they should not simply be labelled 'domestic crime' – which is an indication of how society views women in general. In fact, while there have been advances in international law to address gender-based violence, this has not reduced the prevalence of such crimes in transitional settings (Scanlon and Muddell 2009: 17). Addressing this remains at the core of a women-centred discourse on security governance.

Finally, security was 're-imagined' to mean the equal participation of women 'at all levels of political engagement'. This latter point is critical because the study found that although women have played a key role in contributing to civil society activism as agents of transformation, they 'remain marginalised from the institutions of post-conflict transition' which continue to be heavily dominated by males (Hamber et al 2006: 498–9). Security therefore requires removing restrictions and replacing them with a discourse on equity (meaning fair treatment and opportunities for both men and women) in transitional processes (Meintjes 2001: 73).

The views of the women in the Hamber study underscore the need for transitional processes to provide opportunities for women to articulate alternative perspectives that 'promote a fundamental transformation of security'. Such an approach could result in gender equality 'at all levels of security dialogue'; more than this, it would ensure that gender is a 'central consideration of all domestic and international actors, in all fields relating to the discussion, promotion and provision of security' (Hamber et al 2006: 500).

One can rephrase the point. The re-imagined security of women encompasses a wide reconceptualisation of security to include physical, social, economic and sexual security. When understood in this way, any policy response would necessarily entail bringing together all the relevant institutions to guarantee women's security (Ni Aoláin 2009: 3). In this way, security sector reform would be linked to a broader project of societal and democratic transformation (Ni Aoláin 2009: 3). This re-imagining would not limit the discourse to narrow discussions of civil–military relations nor democratic control of armed forces (from which women are generally excluded). Furthermore, a re-imagined conceptualisation of security would entail a rethink by policymakers as to who the beneficiaries of security sector reform are; this would in turn require rethinking who should participate in and take ownership of the security governance discourse.

It is nevertheless a reality that women and other vulnerable groups remain marginalised and seldom constitute a large enough body among the various groups that engage in 'security sector conversations', namely governments, the security apparatus, local stakeholders (which themselves often constitute an elite body that is not necessarily representative of all civil society groups), and external partners (who tend to promote the traditional model of security reform) (Ni Aoláin 2009: 16).

A major challenge is how to introduce these re-imagined security perspectives into the security discourse during post-conflict reconstruction, thereby ensuring that they have an impact that alters the norms and values that traditionally underpin the security sector. There are instances where women's demands have been heard: significant gains were made in the reform processes in the security sectors of Sierra Leone and Liberia, particularly in Liberia. For example, a special, accelerated learning programme was created to facilitate the recruitment of women into the security sector. As a result, over 300 women were recruited into the Liberian national police force. The first post-war inspector general of police under the new president was a woman (Republic of Liberia Truth and Reconciliation Commission 2009: 24).

But these opportunities do not occur often and are not systematic. As noted above, an approach based on quotas, in which the government guarantees female representation, does not in and of itself lead to a dismantling of patriarchal structures; nor does it change the minds of traditionalists who regard the security sector as the domain of men. A gendered approach requires a re-imagining of the underlying norms, values and perceptions of gender roles and must address concerns pertaining to health, economic empowerment, political participation and gender violence in peacetime. Finally, we continue to see that the security governance discourse in many transitional countries has yet to find a solution to widespread cases of gender-based violence. To its credit, the Liberian government created women and child protection units throughout Liberia with a mandate to investigate sexual exploitation and related abuses.

While there have been advances in international law to address gender-based violence, this has not lessened the prevalence of such crimes in transitional settings (Scanlon and Muddell 2009:

17). Addressing this remains at the core of a women-centred security governance discourse. Security sector reform needs to explore the complex relationship between what is often seen as extraordinary violence during times of conflict and ordinary violence during 'peacetime' or in 'post-conflict' contexts. The experience of countries such as Rwanda and South Africa suggests that domestic abuse invariably increases in post-conflict settings.

This raises concerns about the quality of reform in transitional processes and the inability to recognise and respond to past gender abuses. Indeed, institutional reform, including reform of the security sector, is about both redress and reparations (this points to the holistic nature of transitional justice). Weeding out perpetrators from state institutions (through vetting and lustration) should pave the way for building civic trust in a new state security apparatus that is more accountable and more capable of protecting women and other marginalised groups against the return of violence. (This relates to the preventive dimension of transitional justice.) More critically, in order to ensure that the security sector has a broad conceptual understanding of the violence experienced by women, a transformative agenda should subvert the 'militarised view of what constitutes safety' and replace it with a concept that allows the security sector to respond with transformative actions that address what is seen as 'ordinary' violence in a more meaningful way. The fact that gender-based violence is still so prevalent raises questions about the extent to which transitional justice measures can usefully contribute to meeting women's security concerns in various transitional settings.[5]

Conclusion: the impact of transitional realities

This chapter has focused on the gains and opportunities that can be attained if a gendered transitional justice approach, and specifically a gendered security sector approach, were incorporated into the various transitional processes. However, when judged against realities on the ground (as the case studies in this book demonstrate), many of these gains are ad hoc; they are not part of any systematic process. This leads us to conclude that years of campaigning for the inclusion of a women's agenda has not resulted in sustainable gender equality or social transformation.

There are two reasons for reaching this conclusion. First, the transformative potential of transitional justice is often limited by political realities; as a result women's issues or the concerns of ordinary citizens are often sidelined. A reality (and not just on the African continent) is that in transitional periods political elites on either side of a conflict are sometimes the perpetrators. They then negotiate processes that in the end serve to protect their interests and maintain the status quo. Peace agreements and political deals are often aimed at managing or containing transitional situations (to avoid retributive action or the fundamental transformation of societies). Those deals that seem to 'deliver' transitional justice processes are often held hostage by perpetrators of the conflict, who use them as vehicles to either deny or delay transformative change, including securing justice and accountability.

Second, and related to this point, transitional justice has been (and continues to be) slow in broadening its scope to ensure its relevance to the wider transitional processes such as constitutional reform making.[6] As a result, transitional justice advocates often fail to link their goals and objectives to larger processes of political change. In addition, transitional justice has been slow to broaden its scope to incorporate questions of socio-economic justice and structural injustice in its discourse. It needs to do this if it is to properly address questions of redistributive justice. The need for equity is a core demand in the women's agenda. If transitional justice is to realise its potential to transform the lives of marginalised groups, it is necessary to link its project to other parallel processes. In particular it must link its project to demands for social (redistributive) justice, and not just retributive and restorative justice (reparations).

A re-imagined gendered security governance structure demands that transitional justice engages in questions of social justice. A particular focus should be how to overcome pre-existing structural gender inequalities that result in discrimination and the marginalisation of women and other citizens; these inequalities remain embedded in present-day policies. This is a matter that needs to be addressed in relation to constitutional issues, in particular the need to promote equality through a bill of rights (O'Rawe 2009: 3). Advocates for transitional justice must also show how the inequalities of the past remain firmly entrenched in the present.

A women's agenda should prioritise the need to tackle gender-based violence and to deal with questions of economic, social and political security in post-conflict governance structures.

Notes

1. These can include torture, bodily injury, sexual violence, forced recruitment and curtailment of reproductive freedom.
2. Articles 7 and 8 of the Rome Statute of the International Criminal Court.
3. The previous reparations regime was based on the work of the Independent Arbitration Panel, set up in 1999. It had awarded reparations to 3,681 people but faced criticism for arbitrariness and lack of transparency in its operations.
4. A Lebanese respondent from the study noted that women who do not have jobs, who stay at home and are dependent on their husbands to protect them from hunger and poverty, fear physical violence more than women who have jobs and feel more able to confront their husbands when they feel abused (Hamber et al 2006: 498–9).
5. The apparent rise in post-conflict domestic violence may result from a number of interrelated processes. It is increasingly acknowledged that transitional justice has a responsibility to create mechanisms to ensure that violence does not simply move to the home and that a more holistic approach to justice is achieved in societies in transition.
6. In a number of countries where transitional justice mechanisms exist, they were required by constitutional provisions. In some instances, constitutional norms conditioned how these mechanisms would be designed and executed. South Africa is a case in point.

References

Arthur, P. (2009a) 'How "transitions" reshaped human rights: a conceptual history of transitional justice', *Human Rights Quarterly*, vol. 31, pp. 321–67

Arthur, P. (2009b) 'Identities in transition: developing better transitional justice initiatives in divided societies', November, http://www.ictj.org/en/research/projects/research6/index.html, accessed 15 February 2010

Conseil Consultatif de Droits de l'Homme (CCDH) (2008) 'Community reparations: assessment of the first year of launching the programme', *CCDH Newsletter*, Institution National Pour la Promotion and la Protection des Droits de l'Homme, no. 1, August, http://www.ccdh.org.ma/spip.php?article750, accessed 17 October 2009

de Greiff, P. (2010) 'Theorizing transitional justice', in Nagy, R. and Elster, J. (eds) *Nomos, Vol. L: Transitional Justice*, New York, New York University Press

Hamber, B., Hillyard, P., Maguire, A., McWilliams, M., Robinson, G., Russell, D. and Ward, M. (2006) 'Discourses in transition: re-imagining women's security', *International Relations*, vol. 20, no. 4, pp. 487–502

Instance Equité et Réconciliation (IER) (2006) 'Summary of the final report of the Equity and Reconciliation Commission', Casablanca, IER

International Center for Transitional Justice (ICTJ) (2005) 'Transitional justice in Morocco: a progress report', http://www.ictj.org/images/content/1/9/197.pdf, accessed 7 May 2010

International Center for Transitional Justice (ICTJ) (2008a) 'Gender justice', March, http://www.ictj.org/en/tj/786.html, accessed 15 October 2009

International Center for Transitional Justice (ICTJ) (2008b) 'Justice-sensitive SSR', March, http://www.ictj.org/en/tj/783.html, accessed 4 March 2010

Meintjes, S. (2001) 'War and post-war shifts in gender relations', in Meintjes, S., Pillay, A. and Turshen, M. (eds) *The Aftermath: Women in Post-Conflict Transformation*, London, Zed Books, pp. 63–77

Meintjes, S., Pillay, A. and Turshen, M. (eds) (2001) *The Aftermath: Women in Post-Conflict Transformation*, London, Zed Books

Muddell, K. (2009) 'Limitations and opportunities of reparations for women's empowerment', September, http://www.ictj.org/static/Publications/bp_muddell_gender_rev3.pdf, accessed 28 May 2010

Ni Aoláin, F. (2009) 'A preliminary audit of identity and representation in the context of Security Sector Reform, with particular emphasis on Gender', unpublished

O'Rawe, M. (2009) 'Security system reform and identity in divided societies: lessons from Northern Ireland', October, http://www.ictj.org/en/research/projects/research6/thematic-studies/3197.html, accessed 26 February 2010

Republic of Liberia Truth and Reconciliation Commission (2009) *Women and the Conflict*, Appendix 1, vol. 3, pp. 1–112

Rubio-Marín, R. (ed) (2006) *What Happened to the Women? Gender and Reparations for Human Rights Violations*, New York, Social Research Council

Rubio-Marín, R. (ed) (2009) *The Gender of Reparations: Unsettling Sexual Hierarchies While Redressing Human Rights Violations*, New York, Cambridge University Press

Scanlon, H. and Muddell, K. (2009) 'Gender and transitional justice in Africa: progress and prospects', *African Journal on Conflict Resolution*, vol. 9, no. 2, pp. 9-28

Sierra Leone Truth & Reconciliation Commission (SLTRC) (2004) *Witness to Truth: Report of the Sierra Leone Truth & Reconciliation Commission*, Freetown, SLTRC

United Nations (UN) (2007) 'Basic principles and guidelines on the right to a remedy and reparation for gross violations of international human rights law and serious violations of international humanitarian law', adopted and proclaimed by General Assembly Resolution 60/147, 16 December

Urgent Action Fund-Africa et al (UAF-A) (2007) *The Nairobi Declaration on Women's and Girl's Rights to Remedy and Reparation*, 19–21 March

3

Alternative discourses: a feminist approach to re-thinking security

Awino Okech

Introduction

This chapter[1] seeks to articulate three central arguments regarding feminist[2] contributions to security governance discourse and praxis in Africa (Lewis 2006; Muthien, n.d.; Mama 2009; Clarke 2009). The first recognises that state-centric approaches to security do not work for citizens collectively. This is particularly the case in contexts where governance is personalised and patronage constitutes the modus operandi of governing. The experiences of a number of African countries in the last decade – Sudan, Somalia, Rwanda and South Africa – also point to the fact that the traditional view of security as constructed through the lens of protection from an external aggressor has been destabilised by a history of competing internal interests surrounding democratisation and the equitable distribution of national resources rather than large-scale contestations across borders. As such, a response that takes contexts seriously would require a shift in focus inwards. This is a position that is now well established and which has led to the evolution of a human security framework as an alternative to state-centric discourses.

Second, if we take the above as representative of fact, then the history of women[3] as a constituency within the 'African state' must come under scrutiny. The redefinition of security as a concept or the identification of security challenges on the continent today must recognise how previous relationships among both state and non-state actors were constructed, and how they need to be reconfigured for any tangible shifts to occur. While recognising that the history of diverse groups of African women and their relationship to their various nation states is varied, in a sample comprising Algeria, Zimbabwe[4] and South Africa, all contexts where women's participation in and centrality to the liberation movements has been well documented, we notice a pattern. This is the massive reversal of any gains post-independence and a continued pendulum engagement with the state in terms of securing women's rights. Scholars such as McFadden (2002) have argued that these reversals are rooted in the fact that women became a part of the nationalist project as defined and steered by men. As such, their contributions to the post-colonial state-building project were framed through their engagements with 'comrades' and leaders as brothers and husbands, that is by relationships constructed around their perceived innate roles as women, with these structures being maintained after liberation. These reversals occur irrespective of examples of various forms of 'gender bending' that occurred in Zimbabwe or recently in Liberia with regard to alternative femininities emerging in a war context.

Third, in a context, therefore, where the participation of women remains visible and changes are unachievable, and where spaces and power are arrogated in ways that privilege a dominant male ruling elite, any attempts to reconfigure security as a concept and an ideal will be flawed if it does not take seriously a metanarrative of both hegemonic violent masculinities and the public/private dichotomy that informs governance. Indeed, feminist scholars have long noted that the distinction between the personal and the political, or between private and public, is itself a fiction designed to support an oppressive status quo: our most personal acts are, in fact, continually being scripted by hegemonic conventions and ideologies (Butler 1990).

In addressing these three arguments, I take as my point of departure a particular meaning of gender equality, one that centralises women's rights as a minimum for achieving gender equality. This approach recognises that existing inequalities based on class[5] and race are doubly felt by women, who already have to counter a subordinate position owing to societal structures that privilege male power.

The chapter recognises the growing scholarship on masculinities that challenges essentialised discourses around manhood in useful ways, arguing for an approach that surfaces the reality of multiple masculinities subsumed under a hegemonic and often violent one (e.g. see Ratele 2001; 2008). However, this analysis does not fall within the scope of the chapter.

The chapter also takes cognisance of the decades and multiple zones of peace activism by women on the continent that have led to a range of shifts in peace building and conflict transformation work, even those that are not named as such. Since a specific examination of the gains, drawbacks and challenges are ably explored by other case studies in this volume, this chapter does not address this in detail. See the chapters by Ecoma Alaga, Eka Ikpe, Mohammed Sidi Bah and Tim Murithi.

This chapter offers some conceptual considerations that ought to frame reflections on security governance, grounding it in feminist scholarship, while recognising that the literature on the specific zone of women and security is an emerging one in Africa.

An overview of security discourses

Two factors can be argued to have influenced the discourse on security governance on the continent today. Beyond global foreign policy agendas, the first can be seen in the nature and conduct of war in most modern African contexts, which has contributed to shifting traditional perceptions of state security, which is not only about the protection of a state's borders, but also intra-country conflicts. The second, as Bunch points out, is the reality of a post-structural adjustment era where governments' regulatory powers in most contexts are stripped, thus leaving the notion of governments being accountable to citizens for security or any other public good a misnomer (Bunch 2003: 2).

It is important to highlight that the impact of structural adjustment programmes on security and its governance is an indirect one. While much of the social sector – for example, health, education – was increasingly left to the private realm, security was centralised in the hands of the state, albeit unsuccessfully in many cases. Citizens' security invariably suffered the same fate as other sectors in any effort to roll back the state, which focused on security for the few at the expense of the majority (Olonisakin 2009). While a standard security discourse remains dominant in international relations, influenced obviously by foreign policy objectives such as those defining the so-called 'war on terror' and the subsequent development of projects such as African Command (AFRICOM),[6] other ways of imagining security have become more prominent in recent years and represent challenges to institutionalised ways of 'doing security' (Hamber et al 2006: 487).

The institutionalised approach to security may be termed the state security discourse. This approach focuses on the protection of state borders from external threats, or the protection of state authority in the case of intra-state conflict, and it conceives of 'security' as the absence of threat from violent conflict[7] (Hamber et al 2006: 488). The right that state security discourse protects is the right of states to territorial integrity. This is argued to be a militaristic discourse that permits states to monopolise the use of force and limit the participation of civil society in the development of security strategies (Hamber et al 2006: 488). State security discourse imagines that the establishment of political stability in societies beset by conflict will act as a cure for security threats. It gives little attention to security concerns that do not flow from violent conflict and as such is often antithetical to women's security (Hamber et al 2006: 488).

As Edward Newman notes:

> For most people in the world, the much greater threats to security come from disease, hunger, environmental contamination, street crime, or even domestic violence. And for others, a greater threat may come from their own state itself, rather than from an 'external' adversary ... an overemphasis upon statist security can be to the detriment of human welfare needs. (Cited in Hamber et al 2006: 488)

The emergence of the human security discourse in the past two decades, operating alongside the statist discourse, has evolved as an extension of the human development approach that identifies the individual rather than the state as the primary referent of security policy (Hamber et al 2006: 489). Feminist analysts accept as true that patriarchal assumptions and actions privilege men and are globally endemic, although they vary by race, class, culture and ethnicity, among other variables. This notwithstanding, there is consensus that security should be defined by those who are least secure, thus centring women as critical actors in this debate (McKay 2004: 154).

The human security discourse centres around two principles: freedom from want and freedom from fear. Increasingly, most states have gone on to prioritise freedom from fear as a core component of their security sector reform processes (see Hamber et al 2006: 490). In centring freedom from fear as a core component of these debates informing security sector governance[8] interventions, they have focused on sections of the security forces that are viewed as most culpable in a post-war context. As a result, sexual violence and institutions directly responsible for the commissioning of these acts have been key targets.[9] Irregular forces such as vigilante groups and militias who do not operate out of barracks and are only becoming stakeholders in this dialogue peripherally at the state level are not a target of women's rights agencies in their analysis and/or interventions.

Feminist scholars, on the other hand, have argued that the human security discourse fails to fully explore the core issues of bodily integrity (Bunch 2003; Lewis 2006; Muthien n.d.). Not enough attention is paid to the normalised sites of violence that women negotiate daily: the home, the community and the state. Such violence is not only important in and of itself as a by-product of other structural inequalities, but is also connected to the perpetuation of other forms of domination and insecurity in the world (Bunch 2003: 5). In adopting a gender-mainstreaming approach to the human security discourse, Bunch notes that little attention has been paid to women-specific work (Bunch 2003: 4), thus omitting from the human security discourse the issues of violence against women, gender inequality in control over resources, gender inequality in power and decision making, women's human rights, and women (and men) as actors, not victims (Woroniuk 1999).

Body politics: women and the state

Feminist scholars have argued that an understanding of women's participation or lack of it in the state- and nation-building processes must be located within an understanding of sexuality as a paradigm and women's bodies as a part of this (Stoler 2002; McClintock 1995; Burton 1999; Tamale 2005). A feminist-informed approach places the questions of homosexual and heterosexual arrangements and identities as charged sites of (political) tensions and treats sexual matters not as a metaphor for inequities, but as foundational to the material terms on which national building was carried out (Stoler 2002: 14). While dominant theorisations on nations and nationalism[10] have treated gender relations as irrelevant, major schools of nationalism scholars also see nations as natural and universal phenomena that are an automatic extension of kinship relations. Yet discussions on issues of national production or reproduction do not usually relate to women, but instead to state bureaucrats or intellectuals (Yuval-Davis 1997: 22).

The hidden nature of this contribution can in part be attributed to the social contract model of statecraft on which most states continue to be founded and which distinguishes between the public and private spheres. Women and the family are circumscribed to the private domain and not seen as politically relevant (Yuval-Davis 1997: 22). Since nationalism and nations have usually been discussed as part of the public political sphere, the exclusion of women from that arena has contributed to their exclusion from this discourse as well. The validity of the private/public dichotomy model has been variously challenged, with feminist scholars arguing that the public realm cannot be fully understood separately from the private realm. This position destabilises the false dichotomy perpetuated by states to keep certain zones under the control of 'culture', 'tradition' and the church, although, when it suits it, particularly when challenging reproduction, the state crosses into the seeming 'private zone'. This can be seen in African governments' reluctant approaches to implementing effective legislation on violence against women or their fervour at instituting policies linked to the surveillance of women's bodies, such as those relating to the reproductive health rights of women – termination of pregnancy laws are a case in point. A central dimension of these policies is usually to a greater or lesser extent concerned with the 'genetic pool' of the nation. So we will notice that nationalist projects that focus on genealogy and origin as the major organising principles of the national collectivity – under which the vast majority of African conflicts fall – would tend to be more exclusionary than others. For only by being born into a certain collectivity can one be a full member in it. Thus, the control of marriage, procreation and therefore sexuality[11] tends to be high on the nationalist agenda (Yuval-Davis 1997: 22).

The emergence of identity politics as a means of political empowerment among marginalised groups has meant that gendered bodies and sexuality play a pivotal role in marking territories, and reproducing nations and narratives of these nations and other collectivities (Yuval-Davis 1997: 39). Women as the carriers/bearers of collective identity and honour, both personally and collectively, therefore face immense pressure when these collectivities are under threat (Yuval-Davis 1997: 45). Consequently, a variety of cultural, legal and political discourses are deployed in the construction of the boundaries of nations. Nationalist discourse would, for instance, stake out those sexual practices that are nation building and ethnicity and race affirming, marking unproductive eroticism not only as immoral, but also unpatriotic (Stoler 2002: 155). Women's citizenship also becomes an area of regulation, where, on the one hand, they are included in the general body of citizens and, on the other, there are always rules, regulations and policies specific to them (Yuval-Davis 1997: 24).

As biological producers of children/people, women are also bearers of the collective within these boundaries. Often their primary identities within these collectivities override those they have as women (Yuval-Davis 1997). As such, questions have been raised about the possibilities of women being able to dissociate themselves from kinship and ethnic boundaries in order to coalesce into a force that is primarily shaped by their identity as a woman during post-conflict reconstruction processes. Additionally, approaches that take sexuality seriously as an analytical framework have also challenged the potential assumptions of innateness – as linked to reproduction, that is, women as mothers, and particular constructions of femininity and in turn masculinity – as being a useful way through which mobilisation for effective change can occur.

Gender-based violence as a lens

The increasing attention paid by the world community to sexual violence – whether through the hallmark United Nations Security Council (UNSC) Resolution 1325 or through occurrences in the Democratic Republic of Congo (DRC) or Darfur – has generated unprecedented scrutiny of what feminists have long argued to be a daily experience for women. Most of these approaches have involved the deployment of a particular language, such as 'rape as a weapon of war', which focuses the occurrence of rape within the context of conflict as warranting a different kind of attention from the gender-based violence that occurs daily.

While the statistics of daily violence against women are daunting, attention is rarely drawn to them because they fall in the realm of daily criminal acts, as accepted and expected forms of insecurity associated with institutions such as marriage, informal and formal labour zones, and particular constructions of femininity that see women as those who respond to the desire of others, rather than those who actively desire and seek a response (Valji 2007; Meintjes 2004; El Bushra 2008). Consequently, when African governments cohere through scattered one-off responses to such forms of violence, they communicate that these are sites of normalcy to be dealt with on a case-by-case and often ad hoc basis. As such, governments' responses to sexual violence are based on humanitarianism when it occurs in a zone where attention is already focused due to the 'hard' issues of political instability. The response – both human and financial – is derived from a zone of morality, a zone in which women and children are collectively defined as the property of men and one in which the community must be protected from being taken as spoils of war.[12]

Scholars and practitioners working in the area of conflict and transitional justice in particular (Meintjes 2004; Valji 2007) have pointed to the opportunity, however fleeting, that this post-war moment offers in rewriting the women's narrative in the 'new states'. However, examples from post-conflict countries highlight the seemingly easy slippage back to the norm, even when transitional and/or new governments appear to take gender considerations into account. The United Nations Development Fund for Women (UNIFEM), for instance, notes the following with regard to Somalia:

Women were recognized as a 'Sixth Clan' at the negotiations in Arta in 2000 and succeeded in including a 10 percent quota for women in the Transitional National Assembly. Women participated as delegates and observers to the IGAD-led negotiations from 2002 to 2004 and succeeded in passing a 12 percent quota for women in the new National Assembly and a 25 percent quota in the regional assemblies – which have since, regrettably, been largely ignored by clan leaders. (UNIFEM 2006)

The highly successful Women in Peacebuilding Network (WIPNET) campaign[13] in Liberia, discussed in Chapter 4, equally points to the reversals of any gains women had made, particularly in the security sector governance processes. Ecoma Alaga highlights that responses exist. In fact, these are perhaps instructive responses based on UNSC Resolution 1325 that recognise the presence of women, but in terms of structural shifts, the changes remain negligible. Alaga also focuses attention on the difficulties of sustaining the massive mobilisation campaign and energies that the WIPNET campaign achieved in influencing in tangible ways the reform agenda in the country.

It has been argued that the ability of women to make an impact within the spaces designated by UNSC Resolution 1325, or such as those described by Alaga and UNIFEM above, stems from a choice (not a conscious one) by women's organisations not to engage at a strategic level. A shift in this approach would require engaging with the institutions where power is held and, most importantly, getting into the process early with a clearer 'blueprint' for the change that is not reliant only on the cessation of violence against women and the provision of seats for women within relevant structures.

This argument has its merits. Bennett recognises that:

[h]istorically, many women's organizations have been drawn into service delivery and into a very particular relation to the state (one of lobbying, seeking legal reform or action, and creating alliances with actors such as police, housing departments, educationalists). Such work is essential, but often leaves little time for the vital conceptual and strategic work of building a movement across political constituencies and issues, while still retaining a feminist platform. (Bennett 2008: 5)

If we take as valuable the previous conceptual work on the centrality of body politics to the formation of nations and states (Thomas 2005; Stoler 2002; Yuval-Davis 1997; McClintock 1995), it becomes evident that approaches that seek to 'reorder' society and rethink what security should encompass must centralise the body. A critical engagement with gender-based violence offers such an opportunity, for to do so implicates ideology, structures and systems on which the institutions of the family, the community, the market and the state are founded.[14] Bennett (2008) reminds us nonetheless that discourses on the body and sexuality are so intricate and deeply naturalised within discourses of nationalism, the family, and – indeed – 'being human' that women's organising through the recognition of sexuality as a political force has been challenging. She continues:

> The terms in which 'sexualities' become introduced into legal and political terrain remain contested – it is easier to insert conceptions of 'sexuality' into frameworks of health than it is to discuss sexualities as sources of empowerment; constraint and 'management' within a larger political[15] framework such as those of militarism and nationalism. (Bennett 2008: 2)

Some conceptual considerations

Dominant approaches by women's organisations have not sufficiently engaged with the fact that sexual and other forms of violence against women depend on dichotomised gender identities, in this instance masculinities that reward physical ability, self-control, professionalism, sociability and heterosexuality, contrasting them with images of 'otherness' such as femininity and homosexuality (Clarke 2009: 8). Clarke focuses on an understanding of masculinities as offering a route into effective responses to the question of violence against women, in addition to framing an engagement on women and peace building. This connotes a response that embeds the reconstruction of femininities and masculinities[16] as a means of not only destabilising hegemonic violent masculinities, but also one that redefines notions of weakness, particularly ideas of respectability that influence and shape the potential for transformative women's leadership. This first approach emphasises the need for the redistribution of power.

The second approach evokes the potential of women's innate attributes – mothers, sisters and wives – as offering a space within which to learn – this is with regard to local knowledge on peace building – but also a space for subversion. As a zone that the state opportunistically sees as private, it therefore offers, if you will, a revolutionary space that will not be surveyed in the same way as women-led processes that foreground a political identity. This may include, for example, the opportunity offered through the 'Sixth Clan' in the Somali peace process. In effect, what was proposed was a reification of matriarchies as spaces within which women were peaceful and engaged in particular ways with ideas of power and governance, ways that prioritised cooperation rather than struggle. This approach can be contested on many levels, one of these being its unsustainability when women 'need to be taken seriously', but also because it does not recognise multiple femininities.

A third approach involves scholars who question whether the emergence of feminist human security discourse 'is a good enough answer to the militarization of people's minds that's rapidly becoming "normal" thought' (Petchesky 2002). This is a position that Hamber et al concur with, arguing that:

> [i]t is not simply a question of mainstreaming but rather imbuing an alternative discourse that attempts to redefine our perceptions and understanding of security and where priorities shift from mere 'threat perceptions' and 'deterrence' vocabularies, to a language that takes cognizance of 'structural challenges' and 'enabling spaces'; a priority that we are yet to centre within ongoing security governance processes. (Hamber et al 2006: 500)

The ability to do this within a framework where gender relations are strongly underwritten by patriarchy seems dubious at best. Over the past four decades, considerable energy has been vested in the struggle to hold states accountable to ideals of 'gender equality' (Mama 2008). However, the increasing fragmentation of most African states raises questions about how worthwhile this approach is.

Two thoughts in closing: the first concerns the meaning of the state in Africa. A majority of African states (Kenya, Zimbabwe,

Nigeria, Uganda) as they are presently constituted are neither transitional nor currently constituted as spaces for equal engagement by their citizenry.[17] They are captured spaces, where patriarchy, nationalism and now militarism continue to be redeployed to re-embed structural inequalities while seeming to open a few doors such as those that emerge through legislative gains.[18] The main doors that offer real opportunities to re-imagine gendered relationships and inform a new vision of what 'nation' means remain locked. In essence, the same structures are used to rebuild the 'transitioning' state. A refocus on how nationalism and patriarchy have been deployed in the nation-building process must be the larger starting point for how we begin to rewrite women's narratives.

The second involves troubling the notion of gender. There are those who consider this symbolic order of patriarchy inevitable and ratify patriarchy as an inevitable structure of culture and, as such, see sexual difference as inevitable (Butler 1990: 270). There are others who find this structuralist paradigm useful because it charts the continuing power differential between women and men in language and society and allows us to understand how deeply it functions in establishing the symbolic order in which we live (Butler 1990: 270). Scholar activist Abbas,[19] in the same vein as other feminist scholars before her (see Butler 1990 and Rubin 1975), has argued for the reconsideration of approaches that seek to redistribute power within what is already a constraining construct – gender.

Rationalisations surrounding the currency given to the concept of gender, some of which are more plausible than others, centre on the relational character of gender that connotes women and men (Lazreg 2002: 133). The concept of gender enables us to think of masculinity and femininity as historically and culturally variable rather than fixed by nature, but it also denotes a hierarchical relationship between women and men, not merely the differences between them (Rubin 1984: 282).

It is important to understand how the terms of gender are instituted, naturalised and established, but also to trace the moments where the coherence of the categories is put into question and where the very social life of gender turns out to be malleable and transformable (Butler 1990: 270). This requires a move from claiming rights within the parameters of cultural prescriptions about women's roles and bodies. It is not simply about gender and sexuality as self-evident categories, but about their capacity as contingent and highly unstable systems of power to interrupt, if not to thwart, (security) regimes.

Gender-based violence provides an under-utilised framework to unpack the formalisation of insecurity in the state through the social and bureaucratic institutions of patriarchal states. In using this lens, we also contribute to destabilising gender as a social and hierarchical category with currency. To do so would necessitate the transformation of the institutions based on that hierarchical relationship (the family, the state) that perpetuate women's insecurity, thus inhibiting the transformative potential of governance frameworks.

Notes

1. Parts of this chapter constitute a paper entitled 'Transitioning for Conflict?' commissioned in 2009 by Urgent Action Fund-Africa.
2. I distinguish here between women's organising as a broad, politically undifferentiated space and feminist epistemology that seeks to understand the nature of gender-based oppression and a feminist movement that works towards securing women's rights in various spheres of society.
3. Taking cognisance of the fact that a homogeneous entity of this nature does not exist, but for the purposes of making my point I will proceed briefly with this generalisation.
4. Zimbabwe presents fairly well-documented narratives of women as actors within the liberation movement. While overtures were made about political space, this was also accompanied by immense societal stigma, propaganda and silences associated with women in the liberation movement (Lyons 2004).
5. In reference to the inherent economic disparities that accompany class positions in various African contexts.
6. AFRICOM is a project of the US government that is argued to be geared towards 'ensuring security and interventions to prevent war and conflicts', which when fully operational should have military bases across 53 countries in Africa. This position has, however, been contested, with many scholars arguing that it is yet another strategy by America for using military power against states that 'threaten US national security'. AFRICOM operates with little oversight from the US Congress or international bodies such as the United Nations (see Kidane 2008).
7. The inability of post-conflict states to maintain this narrow definition of security is evident. A majority of these fragile states are unable to extend

their authority to the whole territory (e.g. the DRC, Sudan), thus creating space for the emergence of other non-state security actors.

8. Core security institutions comprise armed forces, police, paramilitary forces, coast guards, militias and intelligence services. Security sector oversight bodies include the legislatures and legislative committees; ministries of defence, justice, foreign affairs and internal affairs; the office of the president; and financial institutions. Non-core security institutions include the judiciary; customs; correctional services; other uniformed bodies and non-statutory security forces (i.e. liberation armies, guerrilla groups, traditional militaries, political party security forces and private security organisations).

9. Which for organised units across the continent have been the military and/or peacekeeping forces.

10. Gellner (1983: 1, 36) defines nationalism as a theory of political legitimacy that requires that ethnic boundaries should not cut across political ones and in particular that ethnic boundaries within a given state should not separate the power holders from the rest of the people, and therefore state and culture must somehow be linked.

11. The increasing focus on promoting marriages across the ethnic divide in Kenya as a means of creating national cohesion also point to the ways in which women's reproductive capacities are used as mechanisms to either 'save' or entrench particular narratives on identity as a mobilising force. The examples of Rwanda and South Africa point to contexts where overt and covert policies on miscegenation were deployed liberally as mechanisms to maintain the national gene pool and where women became targets.

12. In line with provisions of the Geneva Convention.

13. Whose success led to the movie *Pray the Devil Back to Hell*.

14. See OHCHR (n.d.).

15. The author is currently concluding a doctoral thesis that explores the intersection between culture and nation-state politics and argues for the need to pay keener attention to cultural practices, particularly in contexts where resources and power are contested via identity (ethnicity or race).

16. Scholarly and programmatic work on masculinities today and those on women and militarism, for instance, both focus on the need to rethink how both femininities and masculinities are constructed. For the former, this means destabilising hegemonic violent masculinities as the only type of manhood that exists and bringing to the fore approaches that focus on other 'types' of men (see the work of Sonke Gender Justice, for instance). For the latter, the work of recognising that not all masculinities are violent is slowly gaining ground in terms of thinking through what it means to build alliances across political spaces, but attempts to engage in this way today are also clouded by increasing resource challenges around work on gender equality. Increasingly, money is being targeted at projects working with men or those that emphasise male involvement, to the detriment of work specific to women's rights. While there is some useful work by male allied agencies working on gender equality, there is a range of opportunistic ones such as Maendeleo ya Wanaume in Kenya.

17. Bosire (2006) speaks to the rhetoric of women's equality that is utilised in an essentialist manner and not necessarily to redress inequalities by states in 'transition', and to the nature of African democracies today and the recycling of old guards into new democratic movements.

18. I do not argue in any way that these gains are not important. Quite the contrary – these gains must be celebrated as contributing to significantly improving women's participation in public spaces and accessing resources. However, as all the authors in this volume underscore, this is not sufficient.

19. Abbas (forthcoming) specifically speaks to the limitations of African feminist movement approaches that focus on redistributing power, with gender as a primary construct, which hinders the potential linkages with and/or the emergence of a strong African queer movement.

References

Abbas, Hakima and Ekine, Sokari (eds) (forthcoming) *An African Queer Movement: Considering LGBTI Activism in Africa*, Oxford, Pambazuka Press

Bennett, Jane (2008) *The Challenges Were Many: The One in Nine Campaign in South Africa*, Toronto, AWID

Bosire, Lydiah (2006) 'Overpromised, underdelivered: transitional justice in sub-Saharan Africa', http://www.ictj.org/static/Africa/Subsahara/AfricaTJ3.pdf, accessed 1 June 2010

Bunch, Charlotte (2003) 'A feminist human rights lens on security', http://www.cwgl.rutgers.edu/globalcenter/charlotte/humansecurity.pdf, accessed 28 June 2010

Burton, Antoinette (ed) (1999) *Gender, Sexuality and Colonial Modernities*, New York and London, Routledge

Butler, Judith (1990) *Gender Trouble: Feminism and the Subversion of Identity*, New York, Routledge

Clarke, Yaliwe (2009) 'Security sector reform: a reflection on women's activism in Africa', paper presented at the Pan-African Conference on Sexual and Gender-Based Violence, 'Due Diligence and Women's Security: Relocating the Narratives', Kampala

El Bushra, Judy (2008) 'Feminism, Gender, and Women's Peace Activism', in Cornwall, Andrea et al (eds) *Gender Myths and Feminist Fables: The Struggle for Interpretive Power in Gender and Development*, Oxford, Basil Blackwell

Gellner, E. (1983) *Nations and Nationalism*, Oxford, Basil Blackwell

Hamber, B., Hillyard, P., Maguire, A., McWilliams, M., Robinson, G., Russell, D. and Ward, M. (eds) (2006) 'Discourses in transition: re-imagining women's security', *International Relations*, vol. 20, no. 4, pp. 487–502

Kidane, Nunu (2008) '"Africa COMMAND" spells colonialism', Priority Africa Network, 6 October, http://www.stwr.org/africa/africa-command-spells-colonialism.html, accessed 28 June 2010

Lazreg, Marnia (2002) 'Development: feminist theory's cul de sac', in Saunders, K. (ed) *Feminist Post-development through Rethinking Modernity,*

Post-colonialism and Representation, London, Zed Books

Lewis, Desiree (2006) 'Rethinking human security: the implications for gender mainstreaming', in Hendricks, Cheryl (ed) *From State Security to Human Security in Southern Africa: Policy Research and Capacity building Challenges*, monograph no. 122, Pretoria, Institute for Security Studies

Lyons, Tanya (2004) *Guns and Guerilla Girls: Women of the Zimbabwean National Liberation Struggle*, Trenton, NJ, Africa World Press

Mama, Amina (2008) 'Editorial', *Feminist Africa: Militarism, Conflict and Women's Activism*, vol. 10, Cape Town, African Gender Institute

McClintock, Anne (1995) *Imperial Leather*, London, Routledge

McFadden, Patricia (2002) 'Becoming post colonial: African women changing the meaning of citizenship', paper presented at Queens University, Canada

McKay, Susan (2004) *Women, Human Security and Peace Building: A Feminist Analysis*, IPSHU English Report Series no. 19, http://www.hegoa.ehu.es/congreso/bilbo/doku/bost/humansfeminist, accessed 28 June 2010

Meintjes, Sheila (2004) 'Fostering political accountability through "truth and reconciliation": civil responsibility and engagement between state and society in South Africa's post apartheid democracy', in Coomaraswamy, V. and Fonseka, D. (eds) *Women, Peacemaking and Constitutions*, New Delhi, Women Unlimited

Muthien, Bernadette (n.d.) 'Engendering security', http://www.glow-boell.de/media/de/txt_rubrik_3/Muthien_autorisiert.pdf, accessed 2 May 2010

Office of the High Commissioner for Human Rights (OHCHR) (n.d.) *15 Years of the United Nations Special Rapporteur on Violence against Women, Its Causes and Consequences*, http://www2.ohchr.org/english/issues/women/rapporteur/docs/15YearReviewofVAWMandate.pdf, accessed 17 April 2010

Olonisakin, 'Funmi (2009) 'Women and the governance of security and development in Africa', paper presented at the Pan-African Conference on Sexual and Gender-Based Violence, 'Due Diligence and Women's Security: Relocating the Narratives', Kampala

Petchesky, Rosalind (2002) 'Violence, terror, and accountability: reports from the field', paper presented at the National Council for Research on Women Annual Conference, 'Facing Global and National Crises: Women Define Human Security', New York

Ratele, K. (2001) 'Between "ouens": everyday makings of black masculinity', in Morrell, R. (ed) *Changing Men in Southern Africa*, Pietermaritzburg, University of Natal Press/London, New York, Zed Books

Ratele, Kopano (2008) 'Analysing males in Africa: certain useful elements in considering ruling masculinities', *African and Asian Studies*, vol. 7, pp. 515–36

Rubin, Gayle (1975) 'The traffic in women: notes on the "political economy" of sex', in Reiter, Rayna R. (ed) *Toward an Anthropology of Women*, New York, Monthly Review Press

Rubin, Gayle (1984) 'Thinking sex: notes for a radical theory of the politics of sexuality', in Carole, Vance (ed) *Pleasure and Danger: Exploring Female Sexuality*, Boston, Routledge

Stoler, Anne Laura (2002) *Carnal Knowledge and Imperial Power: Race and the Intimate in Colonial Rule*, Los Angeles, University of California Press

Tamale, Sylvia (2005) 'Eroticism, sensuality and "women's secrets" among the Baganda: a critical analysis', *Feminist Africa: Sexual Cultures*, vol. 5, Cape Town, African Gender Institute

Thomas, Lynn (2005) *Politics of the Womb: Women, Reproduction and the State in Kenya*, Kampala, Fountain

UN Development Fund for Women (UNIFEM) (2006) 'Beyond numbers: supporting women's political participation and promoting gender equality in post-conflict governance in Africa', http://www. womenwarpeace.org/unifem/framework/publications, accessed 24 April 2010

Valji, Nahla (2007) 'Gender justice and reconciliation', *Dialogue of Globalisation Occasional Paper*, no. 35, November, Nuremburg, Friedrich Ebert Stiftung, http://library.fes.de/pdf-files/iez/05000.pdf, accessed 2 June 2010

Woroniuk, Beth (1999) 'Women's empowerment in the context of human security: a discussion paper', background document for the Joint Workshop of the UN Inter-Agency Committee on Women and Gender Equality and the OECD/DAC Working Party on Gender Equality on Women's Empowerment in the Context of Human Security, Bangkok, Thailand, 7–8 December

Yuval-Davis, Nira (1997) *Gender and Nation*, London, Sage

Part 2
Country case studies

4

Security sector reform and the women's peace activism nexus in Liberia

Ecoma Alaga[1]

Introduction

Liberia is a country in transition from war to peace. The end of the prolonged 14-year war (1989–2003) and the journey towards post-conflict recovery were made possible by a number of interrelated activities by a number of agencies and actors, on separate tracks but with a common agenda. These activities broadly ranged from peacemaking and peacekeeping to peace building and were initiated and undertaken both locally and internationally. One of the key agencies that was actively and visibly engaged in targeted action at both community and national levels to bring about a cessation of violence and initiate the process of post-conflict recovery was the Liberian women's movement. This movement was active both within the country and in the diaspora. Its systematic and sustained peace activism in Liberia and Ghana (the location for the 2003 peace talks) contributed to broader initiatives and efforts that facilitated a ceasefire and the deployment of both a regional and a United Nations intervention force. Through these efforts the warring parties were brought to and kept at the negotiation table. This culminated in the signing of a Comprehensive Peace Agreement (CPA). This in turn created favourable conditions for the installation of a National Transitional Government of Liberia. This paved the way for the holding of the 2005 elections, which brought Africa's first elected female president to power.

The process of post-war recovery and reconstruction in Liberia is ongoing and includes a variety of longer-term initiatives to address widespread political, socio-economic, environmental and security problems. These are direct consequences of the country's protracted war experience and also the root cause of its present human security challenges. The reform of the country's security sector is a crucial aspect of Liberia's post-conflict recovery process because of its relevance to an emerging democratic polity, good governance, the rule of law, gender justice and sustainable peace and security. The expectation is that this reform process will enhance institutional efficiency and accountability and ensure the delivery of security and justice to the state, its people and communities. It is hoped that it will ultimately transform security governance for the benefit of ordinary citizens, particularly the women of Liberia whose collective action for positive change in the midst of a complex situation helped to bring about the current political dispensation.

This chapter provides an overview of two contemporary developments in Liberia: the emergence of women's active and visible role in peace building on the one hand and security sector reform (SSR) on the other. The chapter examines the trajectory of, and extent to which, the lessons from the Liberian women's peace activism (2003–05) are linked to present-day national security discourse, policymaking and practice. It will also examine and analyse the origins and practice of SSR in Liberia and explore the extent to which the Liberian women's agenda has informed the structure and processes of the emerging security system in Liberia. Overall, the chapter provides insights through case studies of mainstreaming women's issues in Liberia and the gender agenda in the post-conflict SSR processes.

Context

Liberia was ruled by an Americo-Liberian oligarchy at its founding in the mid-1900s. Despite a long history of social and political exclusion, the country enjoyed relative stability until 1979, when riots broke out following an increase in the price of parboiled rice from $22 to $30 per 100 pounds. Liberia's army, law enforcement agents and foreign troops from neighbouring Guinea played a crucial role in quelling this bloody riot, which claimed the lives of

40 people and caused injuries to many more (Tellewoyan 2005). Tensions increased throughout 1979 as the riots drew attention to and sparked hostilities arising from deep-rooted structural concerns, which the Tolbert-led government had inherited from Tubman's 27-year rule.

The root causes of the conflict included economic inequality; violations of human rights; ethnic hatred and rivalry; corruption; mass illiteracy; a skewed system of land tenure, acquisition and distribution; poverty; and over-centralisation of power (resulting in exclusion and marginalisation). Tensions arising from these socio-political and economic concerns and challenges increased in 1980, resulting in the assassination of President Tolbert and the seizure of power by a group of non-commissioned officers led by Thomas Quiwonkpa, Thomas Weh-Syen, Samuel Doe, Harrison Dahn, Harrison Pennue and Nelson Toe (Huband 1998). This junta-led regime, the People's Redemption Council, was headed by Master Sergeant Samuel Doe. The leadership of this junta reflected the ethnic character of the conflict at the time, as most of its members were from eastern Liberia (from the Gio and Khran ethnic groups).

President Doe's regime (1980–90) was characterised by increased tensions; human rights violations (including arbitrary killings, arrests, detention, beatings and the dismissal of academics and students in particular); the banning of all protest activities (in 1982) on the grounds that these gatherings were being used to breed socialists; the drafting and approval of a new constitution for the second republic; attempted counter-coups; corruption; ethnic cleansing (targeted at the Gio ethnic group); an increase in gender-based crimes against women (especially rape); displacement; decayed infrastructure; ineffective public institutions; deterioration of the rule of law; nepotism; and economic hardship. The 1985 general election, which was intended to return Liberia to civilian rule, was rigged in favour of Samuel Doe (and his National Democratic Party of Liberia), and Doe was inaugurated president of Liberia on 6 January 1986. Three years later, in 1989, civil war erupted when an insurgent group, the National Patriotic Front of Liberia (NPFL), led by Charles Taylor, invaded the country from neighbouring Ivory Coast.

First phase of the Liberian civil war (1989-97)

The country's turmoil did not abate with invasion of the Taylor-led force (Taylor claimed the incursion was aimed at overthrowing President Doe's dictatorial regime). In fact, the NPFL committed massive human rights violations against the Liberian people. The NPFL abducted and enlisted hundreds of child soldiers (including young women) and killed hundreds of unarmed civilians. The country's security apparatus, the armed forces, Executive Mansion Guard, Special Anti-Terrorist Unit, the national police force, and the Special Security Service (among others) were responsible for perpetrating crimes and violence against the citizenry. In addition, the NPFL was reported to have executed a number of its own foot soldiers without trial (Tellewoyan 2005). By 1990, the situation in Liberia had become so alarming, with the proliferation of rebel groups engaged in dreadful acts, that a military monitoring group, the Economic Community of West African States Ceasefire Monitoring Group (ECOMOG) was deployed to intervene in the crisis under the aegis of the Economic Community of West African States (ECOWAS).

There were a number of international initiatives that were aimed at resolving the crisis. In some instances agreement was reached and later reneged upon by the NPFL, for example in 1992 when despite the Yamoussoukro IV Accord the NPFL launched a major assault in the capital city, Monrovia. A series of peace initiatives were launched in 1993 and in July of the same year the Cotonou Peace Agreement was signed between the rebel leaders and the Interim Government of National Unity. The terms of the agreement included the constitution of a new interim government (called the Liberia National Transitional Government), and the parties committed to a ceasefire and the demobilisation of their forces. A United Nations Observer Mission in Liberia (UNOMIL) was established to monitor the terms of the agreement. In September 1993, the Akosombo Accord was signed to augment the Cotonou Accord. This did not, however, bring the crisis to an end: the violence continued amidst further coup attempts, which resulted in the signing of another agreement in Accra in 1994. This agreement was significant in that it incorporated rebel groups not included in the Akosombo agreement. In 1995, the Abuja Accord was signed, establishing a council of state to administer the country until the holding of national elections. A supplement to the Abuja Accord was signed in August 1996 and Ruth Perry became the head of the Liberian National Transitional Government. In 1997 general elections were held and Charles Taylor was inaugurated president, thus bringing an end to the war.

The second phase of civil war (1999–2003)

Taylor's regime was characterised by undemocratic practices including the continued harassment of citizens, executions and corruption. ECOMOG[2] withdrew and Taylor's warlords were transformed into the Liberian army. There was also a proliferation of private security agencies as erstwhile rebel groups transformed themselves. In 2000, an attack was launched on Taylor's undemocratic regime by a rebel movement called Liberians United for Reconciliation and Democracy (LURD), which in 2003 joined forces with the Movement for Democracy in Liberia to call on President Taylor to step down. The emergence of these rebel groups ignited another bout of callous attacks on civilians. Mass killings, looting, abductions, arbitrary arrest, torture and detention, displacement and repression intensified. Women were the targets of rape and other forms of sexual violence. They were abducted and violated even as they searched for food, cared for the sick and elderly, or tried to flee to safety. They were enlisted into the rebel movements, either voluntarily or through coercion (Turshen and Twagiramariya 1998).

It is, however, necessary to state that women were not only victims; they were also part of the combatant (rebel) forces. As the second phase of the war developed and attempts were made by the international community to initiate peace talks, a new movement emerged on the home front in Liberia. This movement comprised Liberian women across all social divides. Under the auspices of a campaign that was called the Liberian Women's Mass Action for Peace, women mobilised and joined forces to say 'never again' to violence and war. Their agenda was explicit and made these demands: an immediate and unconditional ceasefire; the deployment of an intervention force; and the agreement of warring parties to sit at a peace table and negotiate a settlement.

As I will show later in this chapter, the Liberian Women's Mass Action for Peace campaign applied a culturally specific grassroots-based strategy of women's peace activism that over time presented a visible and vocal challenge to militarism and structural violence (Pedersen 2008). In addition, it demonstrated women's indispensable role in building peace and security in conflict and post-conflict environments, as enshrined in the United Nations Security Council Resolution 1325 of 2000 (on women, peace and security).

While it is acknowledged that the women's peace activism campaign which began at the height of the conflict (and continued long after the peace agreement was signed) has contributed to an expansion of political space for women in Liberia, and while women's visibility in political leadership and peace building has increased in the last few years, the post-war debates around security have neither transformed gender relations nor mainstreamed women's issues. This is evident from the ongoing SSR process in post-war Liberia. Despite the obvious inter-linkages between them, this has evolved along a parallel track to Liberian women's peace activism.

The post-conflict period and security sector reform

After 14 years of war, the Comprehensive Peace Agreement (CPA) was finally signed on 18 August 2003 in Accra, Ghana, bringing the total number of peace agreements signed to 17. Following this agreement, Charles Taylor resigned and went into exile. The National Transitional Government of Liberia under the leadership of Charles Gyude Bryant was installed, and in 2005 elections were held, bringing the present administration of President Ellen Johnson-Sirleaf into power. These events altered the political landscape of Liberia and ushered in the difficult, convoluted and politically sensitive process of post-war reconstruction (Jaye 2008). This included peace building, a field in which Liberian women's and civil society groups had become prominent. Post-war reconstruction involved a variety of initiatives. These included reconciliation, healing and the reconstruction of basic social fabric; economic recovery; and the reform and rebuilding of state institutions, including the security sector. The 2003 CPA and the

1996 Abuja Agreement made specific reference to the need to reform Liberia's security sector.

SSR was perceived as fundamental to Liberia's post-war reconstruction process because it was directly linked to good governance, sustainable peace, security and the development of democratic politics both within Liberia and in the ECOWAS sub-region. Thus, the context for SSR in Liberia includes both the local and broader sub-regional security environments. In the first instance, the local context for SSR is one of prolonged authoritarian single-party rule, and this has had a number of dire consequences. These include: cronyism and over-centralisation of power in an 'imperial' presidency (Jaye 2008); undisciplined security sector institutions that have been used as an instrument of political repression and oppression against the very population they were established to protect; defective security oversight because of a weak legislature; a 14-year-long civil war during which the entire security sector became bloated both in sheer size and in terms of its budget; and a factionalised and dysfunctional security sector.

In the second instance, the broader context for SSR in Liberia brought with it various challenges. These were a result of: the growing insecurity in the West Africa sub-region as a result of violent and armed conflict; the proliferation of militia and rebel groups and small arms; increased transnational crimes, including trafficking and sexual exploitation; declining economies, increased poverty, and growing political uncertainty in neighbouring countries such as Guinea and Côte d'Ivoire.

Thus far, the SSR debates and processes in Liberia have, on the one hand, included activities aimed at promoting the efficiency and professionalism of security sector institutions, namely the Armed Forces of Liberia (AFL), the Liberia National Police (LNP) and to some extent the Bureau of Immigration and Naturalisation (BIN), and Rule of Law institutions. On the other hand, these initiatives required a process of national dialogue leading to the drafting of a national security strategy. This was crucial for restoring public confidence in the security sector and for soliciting citizen's inputs. It involved consultation with a wide variety of stakeholders including core security agencies and oversight institutions such as parliament, women's groups and youth groups, civil society, and traditional and religious leaders.

Apart from the initial consultations with role-players across the country on the national security strategy, the SSR process and debates were led largely by external actors. The involvement of nationals in the process has been minimal. With regard to the technical aspects of the reform process, the United States (through DynCorp) and the United Nations Mission in Liberia (UNMIL) have provided training to the army and police respectively. When it comes to governance, the Liberian parliament (particularly its committees on defence and security) has been galvanised to carry out its oversight function as a result of interventions led by the Africa Security Sector Network (ASSN) and its affiliate organisations. These include the Conflict, Security and Development Group (CSDG) at King's College, London; Africa Security Dialogue and Research (ASDR); the Centre for Democracy and Development; and the Geneva Centre for the Democratic Control of Armed Forces (DCAF). National actors that have engaged in the process include the Liberia National Law Enforcement Association and the Civil Society Working Group on SSR.

The level of involvement of women and the integration of gender perspectives in these debates and processes have been unsatisfactory. While some gains have been made in the area of recruitment, especially within the LNP, little has been done to ensure women's active and full participation in the broader processes. In addition, specific issues relating to the protection and promotion of women's rights[3] and the prevention of violence against women have not been an integral part of the discourse. Also, the issue of the prosecution of perpetrators of violence against women (especially those within the security sector) remains unresolved as a result of a number of factors. These include a weak justice system and a culture of impunity. Women's roles in the peace process and in post-war peace rebuilding have not directly influenced security reforms and governance debates and processes; rather, these two processes have evolved separately from each other.

As a result, the security sector institutions that are emerging from these reforms have yet to benefit significantly from the lessons learned from women's engagement in broader peace and security processes in Liberia. The so-called 'reformed' security sector institutions are still predominantly patriarchal and remain insensitive to the security needs of the vast majority of Liberians, especially women. At the technical and institutional levels, women are still grossly under-represented in Liberia's security sector, especially at senior and decision-making levels. At present, the highest ranking position held by a woman within the security sector in Liberia is that of deputy commissioner of the Bureau of Immigration and Naturalisation.

Most of Liberia's security sector institutions lack specific policies on gender and women-related issues, such as sexual violence. Currently only the Liberia National Police has a gender-related policy and this is focused on the mandate of the Women and Children Protection Unit. Except for the LNP, none of the other security sector institutions has a dedicated department, unit or focal point on gender and women-related issues. Sexual harassment and other tacit discriminatory practices are rife within these institutions and there are no appropriate channels for redress. Given the high rate of illiteracy especially among women, current recruitment requirements and procedures do not encourage female enrolment. Though the LNP has taken specific actions to address this by lowering the qualifications for recruitment and launching an accelerated learning programme for female recruits, they are still unable to meet the female recruitment target of 20 per cent. This situation is aggravated by the limited capacity of relevant security sector institutions and their personnel to prevent or respond to sexual violence; they are thus failing to ensure a conducive working environment for women (Malan 2008; Albrecht and Barnes 2008; WIPSEN-Africa 2010).

With regard to gender mainstreaming, most gains have been made in the area of training. Even in this instance, the training has been ad hoc and its content limited to a narrow focus on violence against women, sexual exploitation and abuse, and gender-based violence. Furthermore, the institutional assessments that were conducted within AFL, LNP and BIN (the security sector institutions that have thus far benefited from the SSR process) to guide their respective reform agendas did not engage female staff associations or female personnel as a specific core group.

With regard to the governance component of the security reform debate and practice in Liberia, far less has been achieved. While the capacities of the parliamentary committees for defence and security have been strengthened in the area of security oversight, they are still limited by their lack of focus and expertise on gender and women's issues. Women are still under-represented on these committees and neither committee seeks to consult with women's organisations when executing their law- and policymaking functions. The potential role of parliamentarians in exercising gender-sensitive oversight of security budgets is also largely overlooked in the Liberia parliament. Within the judicial system, women's participation in and their access to the justice system is limited. In addition the capacity of the system to effectively combat sexual and gender-based violence is challenged by a number of factors. These include, for example, gender insensitive laws, competing legal frameworks based on a dual justice system;[4] inadequately trained legal personnel (especially gender-sensitive lawyers and judges); and the functioning of the criminal courts, particularly in the counties.

Given all the above, many rural Liberians have resorted to traditional justice and conflict-resolution mechanisms because of their accessibility, cost-effectiveness and quick closure. However, these traditional mechanisms are largely gender-blind and frequently perpetuate violence and discrimination against women.

Some case studies

This section proffers specific case studies from the Liberian context to illustrate the points made in the previous section. These include, for example, the separate evolution of women's peace activism, and the nature of security reforms and governance processes. The case studies will illustrate the specific narratives that have emerged from both processes, the institutions and actors that have shaped the relevant agendas, and the extent to which transformation in Liberia includes the women's agenda. The chapter concludes with recommendations for change to sustain the transformation.

1 The Liberian Women's Mass Action for Peace campaign

Liberian women bore the brunt of two brutal wars that were characterised by human rights violations, the use of drugs and child soldiers, mass displacement, widespread sexual violence and extreme poverty. Their role in the 14-year war was varied. They were the primary targets of rape and other sexual atrocities that were committed with impunity by both government and rebel forces. They were also political actors, combatants and peace builders. As peace builders, Liberian women engaged in a number of activities – trauma healing, conflict resolution, mediation, campaigning and networking – often at significant risk to themselves (Pedersen 2008).

The role of women in peace building in Liberia gained prominence in the mid-1990s, when the Liberian Women's Initiative (LWI) actively campaigned for an end to the first civil war and participated in the disarmament process. Their strikes, protests and campaigns for greater inclusion of women in the peace process resulted in threats to and harassment of some LWI members by the warring parties. At a West African level, the establishment of the Mano River Women's Peace Network (MARWOPNET) in 2000 reinforced the activities of Liberian women peace builders as they joined forces and collaborated with women peace builders from neighbouring Sierra Leone and Guinea to encourage women's participation in peace processes and demand an end to the violence in Liberia and the region.

With the resurgence of violence in 1999, and based on the lessons that had been learned from MARWOPNET's coalition building, a number of indigenous women's groups in Liberia came together and took a decision to mobilise other women's groups to 'add their voices to those of their sisters in the past in order to bring about change' (Gbowee 2003). Against this backdrop, women mobilised as sisters, wives, mothers, grandmothers, daughters and aunts across all social divides; giving birth to the Liberian Women's Mass Action for Peace campaign. The lead groups involved in the campaign were the Women in Peacebuilding Network (WIPNET) and the Christian and Muslim women's associations. The campaign adopted an ideology called 'women's peace activism', which was based on Galtung's concept of 'positive peace' (Galtung 1996). In other words, this was not only anti-war activism, but also a campaign aimed at the deconstruction of structural forms of violence against women that exist in everyday society. By using women's numerical strength and their ability to mobilise around key issues, the campaign was about more than just ending the war: it was also about transforming deeply rooted patriarchal gender relations that prevented women from playing a central role in formal peace processes and decision making in Liberia.

As indicated previously, the campaign was focused in its message, calling for an immediate and unconditional ceasefire, a fruitful dialogue for a negotiated settlement and the deployment of an intervention force to monitor the implementation of the agreement. At the time, this seemed unrealistic because, as Gbowee and Gautam (2006) noted:

> Our president at the time, Charles Taylor, was against all three! He was a sovereign government, and no one would dictate to him. As a matter of fact, he said the coming in of international peacekeepers was 'terroristic,' and he would not sit and negotiate with 'terrorists', and therefore there would be no ceasefire because the government was duly elected, and he would fight till the last soldier died.

Despite this, the women remained focused. They were exhausted by the war and desperate for change. In a violently divided Liberia, their choice to identify themselves as a collective of Liberian 'women' became key to the success of the movement. The appearance of solidarity was highlighted by the movement's choice of dress. They wore white T-shirts with identical 'lappas' (a traditional cloth wrapped around the torso), without jewellery or makeup, marked only with the WIPNET logo and peace slogans on the back. Their slogan, 'We want peace, no more war!', became a buzz chant.

In order to formalise their actions, the women were issued with WIPNET identification cards, complete with their name and photos. This identification also became a symbol of their individual commitment as they took to the streets and began daily peace vigils at Sinkor airfield in Monrovia. In addition to the sit-ins at the airfield and at displaced persons' camps, their actions included frequent planning meetings to strategise on the next steps, picketing and community mobilisation, and meetings with key stakeholders (including President Taylor, the UN and Guinean embassies, the UN mission, the International Contact Group on Liberia, the parliament and LURD representatives). They also travelled to

Ghana and Côte d' Ivoire where they met with a number of peace-building organisations, religious leaders and women's groups to mobilise support. While in Ghana, they mobilised women (both Liberian refugees and Ghanaian women) to barricade the venue of the peace talks as a strategy to ensure that the warring parties remained at the peace table until a settlement was reached.

It is important to highlight a number of trends that emerged from the mass action for peace campaign. First, when the women appealed to fellow Liberians, the campaign often referred to their status as mothers, wives, daughters, aunts and sisters. This emphasis on their traditional roles worked to their advantage as the stereotype of 'peaceful' and 'non-threatening' women offered them special access to both government officials and the rebel forces. For instance, after several unsuccessful attempts by the women, President Taylor finally agreed to meet them and is quoted to have said, 'Oh I have this terrible flu, but because you are my mothers and I love you all, I had to come down' (Gbowee 2003). This was a double-edged sword as it meant they had to work very hard to be taken seriously. In the current post-war era, this stereotype of women's innately peaceful nature has become problematic as it is used as an argument to keep women from any involvement in 'hard' security matters, including any participation in the SSR process. The SSR should in fact have created the opportunity to consolidate the gains from the women's campaign.

Second, the campaign had to overcome prejudices regarding the social standing of most of its members. Previous women's peace-building movements had been led by organisations such as LWI and MARWOPNET; these generally comprised wealthy, influential and educated women, who claimed they represented the views of the majority of ordinary women in Liberia. In contrast, as a grassroots organisation, WIPNET emphasised the representation and participation of rural women in particular at all levels of the campaign, from community mobilisation, strategy planning, coordination and implementation to decision making. This approach fostered ownership, improved group cohesion and increased confidence and individual levels of commitment for the campaign. It was this sense of ownership that kept the women sitting at an airfield in the rain and sun for months against all odds. In order to sustain this, the campaign rejected a hierarchical organisational structure and adopted a collective decision-making approach. This was highly democratic as women's groups outside Monrovia were involved in the day-to-day decision making via telephone or through their representatives; in this way they were able to support the larger group at the Sinkor airfield. There was no formal leader, although a spokeswoman was appointed to speak for the group.

Third, local ownership of the campaign fostered sustainability. Throughout the campaign, most of the funds were directly generated by the women themselves; this enabled them to prolong the campaign (even after donor support had ceased) until their objectives were attained. This level of dedication affirms the words of Mazurana and McKay (1999), who noted that 'local women are prepared to work and wait longer for results than many donor-imposed project deadlines'.

Fourth, for the women of WIPNET, the campaign had nothing to do with their perceived 'natural' or 'biological' attributes. They were fully aware of the diverse roles women had played in the conflict. Thus, for them, the campaign was an opportunity to transform the status of women and leverage their interests in peace and public decision-making processes. The observer status which their representatives had been accorded at the peace talks in Accra following months of picketing was no longer sufficient. They wanted to be recognised and accepted as key stakeholders in decision making and negotiations. It was against this back-drop that they simultaneously produced their own Golden Tulip Declaration in Accra as the warring parties and government of Liberia signed the CPA. This declaration recalled the principles of the UNSC Resolution 1325 and demanded greater participation for women in the peace process, in the peace-keeping mission to be deployed to Liberia and in the transitional government.

Fifth, the mass action for peace campaign was about movement building. Their adoption of an all-inclusive approach to mobilisation illustrates how movements should and should not be built. A number of points emerge:

- The message was clear and all embracing. Everyone wanted lasting and effective peace; and every single woman who was a part of the campaign acknowledged that this was what they wanted.

- The mobilising factor was (self-evidently) 'womanhood'.
- The approach was highly practical, context specific and appropriate for sustaining the group dynamic.
- There was clear separation of roles and functions. Different working groups were created to deal with welfare issues, communication, logistics, etc.
- The movement prioritised capacity building for its members; consequently the women became familiar with the technical aspects of the peace negotiations over time and were able to influence the outcome of the peace process.
- Networking and partnership building were emphasised and this assisted with resource mobilisation both within and beyond Liberia.

However, there were shortcomings. The movement was narrowly focused and lacked a strategy to sustain the gains once their immediate demands were met. They never deliberated on what the role of the movement would be in post-war Liberia. Consequently, in the aftermath of the war, the movement is now a shadow of its former self. Women are once again reverting to their traditional roles and the gains from mass action have not been maximised to bring about a transformation of the status quo.

Finally, the post-war processes and institutions that emerged failed to prioritise women's issues and their participation. For instance, the mission did not prioritise issues of sexual exploitation and abuse until 2004, when the Office of the Gender Adviser (OGA) was established. In fact, prior to the establishment of OGA, the mission's personnel had themselves been accused of committing sexual offences. Another lesson can be learned from the first phase of the UNMIL-led Disarmament, Demobilisation and Reintegration (DDR) programme in 2003: this failed because it did not engage with Liberians, and with women in particular. As Gbowee observed, 'This failure was based on the UN's failure to obtain local knowledge on many important issues. In consultation with them, we asked them, "Can you get local knowledge?", and they said "no"' (Gbowee and Gautam 2006). This was contrary to the provisions of UNSC Resolution 1325, which requires the UN Department of Peacekeeping Operations (DPKO) to 'ensure that Security Council missions take into account gender

considerations and the rights of women, including through consultation with local and international women's groups' (UNSC
2000: paragraph 15).

In April 2004, during the second attempt at disarmament,
UNMIL's Public Information Office tried to find alternative means
of reaching the ex-combatants. Noting WIPNET's level of organisation and the part they had played in forcing parties to commit
to the peace agreement, UNMIL attempted a new kind of 'door-
to-door sensitisation', and engaged WIPNET as a partner. The
goal was to create awareness amongst the combatants involved in
the DDR package of the need for their involvement in the entire
process. Again as 'harmless and armless' women, the women of
WIPNET appealed to the emotions of the ex-combatants, saying,
'I'm your mother, I'm your sister.' The ex-combatants appeared to
respond positively to the women, appreciating that the message
was coming from members of their own community. As a result
of their engagement, an additional 3,000 combatants benefited
from the process.

However, the experience with the DDR process highlights the
challenge for women peace builders to remain relevant in the post-
conflict period, where women's concerns are considered secondary to 'hard' security issues. As Meintjes et al noted, 'the return to
peace is invariably conceptualised as a return to the gender status
quo, irrespective of the non-traditional roles assumed by women
during conflict' (2001). Yet, as the experience of the Liberian
Women's Mass Action for Peace campaign reveals, there are clear
benefits to sustaining these gains by devising clear policies, concrete strategies and mechanisms for mainstreaming gender issues
and including women's civil society organisations in both 'soft'
(peace building) and 'hard' (security) debates and processes.

2 Gender dimensions of security sector reforms in Liberia

It is undisputable that the role of women in post-war Liberia has
changed. The election of a female president, increased representation of women in cabinet and parliament, the appointment of
many women as deputy ministers, the establishment of a strong
gender ministry and the strengthening of women's civil society

organisations all show that women are participating in the decision-making process in the country (Blunt 2006; Aisha 2005). However, the emerging pattern of women's political leadership is uneven as some sectors seem to have benefited more than others. Liberia's security sector is one where the least change has been made in terms of women's leadership, empowerment and gender equality. The sector is still highly patriarchal and does not consider women's issues a priority.

There have, nevertheless been some achievements in relation to gender and women's issues within the Liberian security sector. Within the Liberia National Police, specific gender-related initiatives have included the provision of gender training for police personnel, the establishment of protection units for women and children within police stations, the deployment of an all-female Indian peacekeeping unit (consisting of 103 women), and the introduction of quotas together with definite enforcement mechanisms, such as the accelerated learning programme to increase female enrolment. The accelerated learning programme entails recruiting female high school dropouts and enrolling them at the Stella Maris Polytechnic. This enables them to obtain the high school certificates, which are a requirement for recruitment into the LNP. While these are positive steps, I would argue that this should only be a 'quick-fix' measure and should be time-bound. Much more attention needs to be focused on girls' education and on transforming discriminatory cultures and workplace environments within security sector institutions.

At the level of the Liberian parliament, a rape bill was enacted in 2003 and a national security strategy, which calls for gender mainstreaming within the security sector, was adopted in 2008. The specialised parliamentary committees on defence and security have also benefited from gender training provided by ASSN, CSDG and the Women, Peace and Security Network Africa (WIPSEN-Africa).

Within the justice sector, a circuit court has been established to fast-track the prosecution of rapists and other sexual offenders. A female judge was also appointed to head the court, and civil society groups, especially the Association of Female Lawyers of Liberia, have been working with female victims of violence to ensure their access to justice. There are claims that gender perspectives have been incorporated into the reform agendas of the Armed Forces of Liberia (AFL) and the Bureau of Immigration and Naturalisation (BIN); however, what this entails remains unclear.

One can argue that, taking everything into account, the gender dimensions of SSR in Liberia have been institution-specific rather than holistic. Even at this level, any change has been ad hoc, fragmented and exclusive of the very women who are supposedly the beneficiaries. It neither followed nor benefited from the methodical approach utilised by the mass action for peace campaign. As a result women receive mixed messages: they are still largely excluded from the reform process and are not involved in crafting the national security policy; there is still a lack of appreciation of their value and function within the security sector; there is very little collaboration between security sector institutions and women's groups, on the one hand, and between female security personnel and women's groups, on the other hand; technical expertise on gender issues within the security sector is inadequate; women's groups and women's institutions, including the gender ministry, are hardly involved in security matters (despite the inclusion of SSR in the Liberia National Action Plan on UNSC Resolution 1325); and there is a high rate of attrition among female security personnel (owing to their low educational standards and the absence of continued accelerated learning programmes for female personnel post-recruitment).

Conclusion

It is clear from the above that the role of women in peace and security and the current SSR process in Liberia has evolved separately. Women's groups seem to be engaged in a struggle to sustain the gains made during their mass action for peace and are seizing different opportunities to achieve this. It is ironic that they have failed to recognise SSR as an opportunity to consolidate their gains and therefore are not involved in the core security sector. For its part, the ongoing SSR process has failed to build on the momentum of the mass action to tap into women's potential. However, it is not too late for the security sector reform process to draw strategic lessons from the mass action for peace campaign; this would benefit the women of Liberia in particular and the country as a whole.

A number of recommendations flow from this chapter. SSR must be led and owned by Liberians. The women, men, girls and boys of Liberia need to collectively assess their security threats and define what should constitute their security agenda. In addition, the security agenda must be all embracing in order to reflect the security needs of the different gender groups. The message should be simple, concise and presented in a language that is understood by all irrespective of status, gender or age.

The agenda development process must promote broad-based participation, and be driven and owned locally. In order to ensure grassroots participation, the process must identify and include specific mechanisms that are accessible to women and men in rural Liberia. The roadmap will need to be reviewed constantly to ensure compliance with set targets. The process must be systematic. However, this is not to say that gender-sensitive security reforms must follow a specific step-by-step approach. What is important is that constituents (at either the institutional or national levels) understand the process so they can contribute optimally and strategise about the next step.

All actors must demonstrate their commitment and support for gender-sensitive security sector reforms. To achieve this, awareness and capacity building must be an integral component of the overall strategy. Security sector institutions, and indeed the entire people of Liberia, will need to be sensitised into appreciating that the full and active participation of women and the incorporation of gender perspectives is crucial for attaining operational effectiveness, for complying with the fundamental principles of equality, non-discrimination and fair play as enshrined in the Liberian constitution, and for ensuring that the security sector is fully representative.

Finally, irrespective of the kind of external support received for the process, security sector reform must respond to the day-to-day security challenges facing the men and women of Liberia. Consequently, it must be context specific and build upon existing indigenous best practices, such as those of the Liberian Women's Mass Action for Peace campaign.

Notes

1. This chapter draws on my first-hand knowledge of the Liberian Women's Mass Action for Peace campaign and my personal involvement in the SSR process in Liberia through my work with the West Africa Network for Peacebuilding and the Women Peace and Security Network Africa (WIPSEN-Africa).

2. The ECOWAS Ceasefire Monitoring Group.

3. 'Rights' here refers to the rights specific to women enshrined in the 2003 Protocol to the African Charter on Human and Peoples' Rights on the Rights of Women in Africa. These include women's right to dignity; to a life of integrity and security; to the elimination of all harmful practices; to equal rights in marriage, separation and divorce; access to justice and equal protection before the law; the right to participation in political and decision-making processes at all levels and spheres; the right to peace; the right to protection in situations of armed conflict; the right to education and training; the right to economic and social welfare; the right to health and reproductive rights; the right to a positive cultural context (at both institutional and societal levels); the right to healthy and sustainable environments; the right to sustainable development; the right to food security and adequate housing; the right of elderly women, women with disabilities and women in distress to special protection.

4. Liberia has a dual justice system, comprising the formal court hierarchy and customary court structures. Although the Liberian constitution provides for the integration of customary justice into the formal system, there are contestations between both systems. The customary system is the preferred system of many Liberians (for both civil and criminal cases) because of its accessibility and effectiveness relative to the formal system. In relation to gender issues, the recent findings of the Legal Working Group reveal that there are aspects of the customary justice system that are at variance with constitutional provisions. For instance, the customary justice systems promote norms and practices that deviate from constitutional and statutory equality rights, particularly those granted to women.

References

Aisha, F. (2005) 'Mainstreaming gender in peace support operations: the United Nations Mission in Liberia', in Aboagye, F. and Bah, A.M.S. (eds) *A Tortuous Road to Peace: The Dynamics of Regional, UN and International Humanitarian Interventions in Liberia*, Pretoria, Institute for Security Studies

Albrecht, P. and Barnes, K. (2008) 'The gender and security sector reform toolkit: civil society oversight of the security sector and gender (Tool 9)', DCAF, OSCE/ODIHR, UN-INSTRAW Publication

Blunt, E. (2006) 'Liberian cabinet posts announced', *BBC News*, 17 January

Galtung, J. (1996) *Peace by Peaceful Means: Peace and Conflict, Development and Civilization*, Oslo, International Peace Research Institute

Gbowee, L. (2003) 'The Liberian Women's Mass Action for Peace campaign', paper presented at the Women in Peacebuilding Network (WIPNET) regional conference

Gbowee, L. and Gautam, S. (2006) 'A conversation with women peacebuilders: Leymah Gbowee and Shobha Gautam', Boston Consortium on Gender, Security and Human Rights, 8 March

Huband, M. (1998) *The Liberian Civil War*, New York, Frank Cass

Jaye, T. (2008) 'Challenges of security sector governance in Liberia', in Olonisakin, F., Alan, B. and Ndiaye, B. (eds) *Challenges of Security Sector Governance in West Africa*, Geneva, DCAF

Malan, M. (2008) 'Security sector reform in Liberia: mixed results from humble beginnings', Pennsylvania, Strategic Studies Institute, US Army War College

Mazurana, D. and McKay, S. (1999) *Women in Peacebuilding*, Montreal, Rights & Democracy

Meintjes, S., Pillay, A. and Turshen, M. (2001) 'There is No Aftermath for Women', in Meintjes, S., Pillay, A. and Turshen (eds) *The Aftermath: Women in Post-Conflict Transformation*, London, Zed Books

Pedersen, J. (2008) 'In the rain and in the sun: women in peacebuilding in Liberia', paper presented at the ISA Annual Convention on 'Violence, Bodies, and Selves II: Conflict, Human Security, and International Politics'

Tellewoyan, J. (2005) *The Years the Locusts Have Eaten: Liberia 1816-2004*, Bridgewater, NJ, Replica Books

Turshen, M. and Twagiramariya, C. (eds) (1998) *What Women do in Wartime: Gender and Conflict in Africa*, London, Zed Books

United Nations Security Council (UNSC) (2000) 'Resolution 1325 on women, peace and security', S/RES/1325 (2000) New York, United Nations Security Council, 31 October

WIPSEN-Africa (2010) 'Report of a gender assessment of security sector institutions in West Africa', Accra, WIPSEN-Africa

5

Sierra Leone: opportunities, challenges and lessons learnt for women

Mohammed Sidi Bah

Introduction

When a country degenerates into armed conflict, as Sierra Leone did from 1991 until the civil war was declared over in January 2002, deep structural instability, which might have been latent or assumed to be part of societal norms, becomes stark. As conflict escalated in the country, the abuse and structural violence previously masked by a facade of peace and stability invariably came to the fore and unleashed themselves in a brutal war and humanitarian tragedy that could not escape international intervention. But notwithstanding the brutality of the war and the untold human suffering it caused, it was an opportunity to create a new order, redress past injustices and unearth the narratives of those, not least women, who were hardly visible to the old system and who suffered disproportionately in wartime.

The 10-year conflict in Sierra Leone witnessed the interplay of state and non-state actors, as well as the massive intervention by the international community. Because of the conflict's complexity and brutal nature, peace was only attainable after a prolonged negotiation process, which culminated in the Lomé Peace Agreement[1] between the government and the Revolutionary United Front of Sierra Leone (RUF/SL), signed on 7 July 1999. The over-riding objective was peace at all costs rather than justice, leading to a blanket amnesty for all the factions, with the sole aim of getting the guns away from the perpetrators to end the war. This, however, did not address the issue of redress for the victims, the majority of whom were women and children who had been deliberately targeted by all the warring factions either as sex slaves or child soldiers. It is estimated that 25.6 per cent of the victims of mass killings were women, while 50 per cent of the country's women were subjected to sexual violence. In part, this weak response to women's rights issues could be attributed to the fact that gender-based violence was considered non-political in the final peace discussions and even though women were at the forefront of the peace movements and prolonged negotiations, they were there as members of male-dominated organisations and institutions.

The transitional justice approaches in Sierra Leone, more specifically the Truth and Reconciliation Commission (TRC), were largely modelled on western concepts and the South African experience. This has not proved to be the panacea for solving the root causes of the war and bringing justice, accountability and restoration to victims. Five years down the line many of the ills that were identified as the main causes of the war are still present, while many of the institutional reforms recommended have not been carried out. The reparations programme is only being implemented more than five years after the TRC report, with a shaky funding foundation, as the United Nations Peace Building Fund (UNPBF) only provided catalytic funding for one year in 2008. It is now emerging that both western and local reconciliation mechanisms should probably be used to achieve justice for voiceless victims, because the latter promote an encounter between the perpetrator and the victim, leading to restoration. Furthermore, the limitation of the mandate of the Special Court for Sierra Leone (SCSL) regarding 'those who bear the greatest responsibility' and the weak judicial infrastructure in the country ensured impunity for the majority of sexual violence perpetrators.

In post-conflict Sierra Leone, therefore, gender inequality still permeates all spheres of social, political and economic life through discriminatory laws, customs, traditions and practices. Various international and national human rights instruments, policies and legislation are in place, but these are ineffective in protecting women, because they are largely inaccessible, unaffordable and unavailable to sexual violence survivors. The current rules of procedure and evidence in respect of crimes of sexual violence are not only discriminatory, but are also offensive to women and girls. The TRC recommendations to abolish discriminatory laws and customs in the areas of marriage, divorce and inheritance have been partially addressed by various parliamentary bills, but its recommendations to address structural inequalities through law reform, access to justice, the abolition of discriminatory customary practices, the building of institutional capacity, and the establishment of educational programmes to counter attitudes and norms that affect women's empowerment are yet to be addressed. In the event, women still continue to be denied access to justice for crimes committed against them during and after the war, as both the formal and informal judicial systems are still male dominated, cumbersome, expensive and intimidating to survivors. Women are also still faced with discrimination in access to productive assets like land rights, credit and the administration of estates, which affects their transformation. The informal justice systems are also subject to customary and traditional influences and prone to interference by traditional, religious and community leaders in favour of out-of-court settlements for sexual offences, which mostly force victims to marry the perpetrators or their parents to accept cash compensation for violent sexual crimes.

Despite women's increased activism on issues of security and justice, these processes have not been aligned with the TRC report's recommendations because of the absence of a government-led and owned implementation programme and action plan, with dire consequences for attracting funds to address women's rights issues and impunity.

This chapter looks at the complex context within which the TRC and SCSL have been implemented in Sierra Leone to achieve justice. An examination of alternative traditional approaches currently under way, lapses in national legislation, pitfalls in efforts made by government and civil society to address sexual violence and impunity will also be assessed. Alongside this, the effect of the non-alignment of reparations with justice and security reforms, and the poor implementation strategy of the reparations programme in addressing sexual violence will also be examined. The chapter also provides case studies and draws conclusions about lessons learnt. The chapter benefits from my first-hand experience in the facilitation of a number of post-conflict initiatives in Sierra Leone, not least as director of the Sierra Leone National Commission for Social Action (NaCSA) until 2008.

Post-conflict Sierra Leone

The TRC process was conceived within the context of a collapsed state characterised by a weak government that was 90 per cent dependent on donor resources and personnel, a non-existent or weak judicial and security apparatus, a fragile peace and eroded social capital. A cash-strapped government in this scenario could not be expected to undertake the resettlement, reconstruction and rehabilitation of ex-combatants, internally displaced people and refugees and at the same time meet the huge cost of reparations. Because of the government's dependence on donors, it was therefore inevitable that the international community would greatly influence the peace process, and in fact it played a major role in determining the agenda and subsequent transitional justice mechanisms, key to which were the TRC and later the SCSL. These were informed by western concepts and practices of reconciliation and justice modelled on the South African TRC experience, which was widely seen as the key to 'finding a definitive settlement to the fratricidal war in Sierra Leone, and the frantic desire to achieve lasting peace, national unity and reconciliation' (TRC 2004). As a new phenomenon, there was no agreement or clarity on the concept of a TRC and, even more so, on reparations.

The very comprehensive TRC report contained recommendations 'to address impunity, respond to the needs of the victims, promote healing and reconciliation and prevent a repetition of the violations and abuses suffered' (TRC 2004). It raised expectations from the various stakeholders – victims, communities, government, civil society and the international community – that could only be met in an ideal situation. It is not surprising that five years down the line many of the ills that were identified as the main causes of the war are still present, while many of the reforms recommended have not been undertaken. SGBV is on the increase, Sierra Leone is still at the bottom of the UN Human Development Index, youth unemployment is still high, the judicial and constitutional reforms are slow, child labour is rampant, officials are not vetted, court trials are delayed, prison conditions are poor, and so on. Does this indicate lack of government ownership of and commitment to the TRC recommendations? To a large extent, it does, given its dependence on donor funds to implement them and because of its different political agenda. Due to these shortcomings, the government's role in justice and reconciliation, especially at the individual level, is therefore highly questionable.

In particular, women continue to face gender-based violence in various forms – physically, sexually and psychologically, ranging from rape to wife battering; unlawful carnal knowledge; early and forced marriage; denial of property rights; female genital mutilation; abandonment; verbal abuse; and the denial of food, healthcare and education to girls. In general, customs and traditions, stigma, ignorance of basic human rights and discriminatory practices against women, insufficient awareness of the new provisions in the gender and child rights laws, lack of adequate resources to operationalise the frameworks and policies acceded to and domesticated by the state, the under-representation of women in the justice and other governance institutions, poverty, the lack of free legal advisory services, the lack of specialised training for the judiciary and police, and gaps in the national legislation are some of the main barriers to access to justice for survivors of gender-based violence.

In response to these deficiencies within the formal and informal judicial systems, there emerged a vibrant group of women's rights activists and civil society coalitions who have been able to put women's rights issues high on the agenda of the justice and security reform processes in the country. Supported by donors and the UN, they have been successful in highlighting access to justice for survivors of gender-based violence and the empowerment of women economically, politically and socially as fundamental to the peace consolidation processes. They have been able to push through gender-sensitive bills and policies, and have achieved the ratification and domestication of international instruments protecting women's rights and the operationalisation of some of them within the security and judicial systems. These include domesticating the principles of the Convention on the Elimination of all Forms of Discrimination Against Women; the African Union Protocol on Women's Rights; the Beijing Platform of Action; the

International Convention on Economic and Social Rights; UN Security Council Resolution 1325; the Rome Statute; and the UN High Commissioner for Refugees Guidelines on Sexual and Gender-based Violence against Refugees, Returnees and Displaced Persons. These are embodied in the Domestic Violence Act 2007, the Devolution of Estate Act 2007, the Registration of Customary Marriages and Divorce Act 2007 and the Child Rights Act 2007.

These instruments have provided space for civil society, especially women's rights groups, to hold government accountable for gender-based violence, mobilise women activists at all levels, document violations, undertake campaigns and implement programmes. Government commitment in terms of resources is low, so there is a heavy reliance on donor funding, which is increasingly drying up. There is a national coordinating body, chaired by the Ministry of Social Welfare, Gender and Children's Affairs (MSWGCA), which has been able to develop an action plan for combating violence against women and girls.

The Justice Sector Reform Secretariat is also enhancing the capacity of the judiciary to dispense justice more speedily by refurbishing, equipping and staffing court houses destroyed during the war, reviewing the penal code system with the aim of removing archaic laws from the statute books, and strengthening national laws to address gender-based violence. For instance, there is no definition in the national laws of crimes against humanity, war crimes and torture, while the Rome Statute was not incorporated in the SCSL's mandate. In addition, there are still impediments to victims accessing justice, as the procedures in the formal judicial systems are costly, highly bureaucratic and elitist, while in the informal system there are strong cultural, traditional and religious pressures from various actors within the male-dominated society for the out-of-court settlement of gender-based violence cases.

There have been institutional reform initiatives such as the retraining of the Sierra Leone Police Force and the establishment of the Family Support Unit (FSU) to prosecute cases of gender-based and other violence against girls and Rainbow Centres to provide support to rape victims. The Prisons Department is also undergoing reforms through capacity building, refurbishment, the separation of girls and women from men prisoners and juveniles from adults, increased access to female prisoners by the International Committee of the Red Cross and civil society groups, and judicial sector review.

Vibrant civil society groups and activists have also emerged, such as the Mano River Women's Peace Network, the 50/50 Group, the Forum for African Women Educators, Help a Needy Child, the Network of People Living with HIV/Aids, Women in Crisis and the Voice of Women. With the emergence of these women's rights organisations and institutions, effective partnerships and coalitions have been forged at various levels that provide opportunity for accessing funds from well-resourced non-governmental organisations (NGOs), the UN and other donors to commemorate major women's rights and HIV/Aids days and implement women empowerment projects involving the provision of skills training, microcredit and enterprise grants, healthcare, childcare and psycho-social counselling.

Women's groups have also played a major role in various campaigns, such as Women Won't Wait and Violence Against Women and Girls. They have lobbied government to ratify and bring into operation international instruments that protect women's rights and have monitored violations of women's rights in the country. Although they are yet to succeed in getting 30 per cent women representation in all political parties and 50/50 women representation in Parliament, women representation has increased in Parliament, local councils, the security forces and the judiciary. The first female chief justice and army brigadier have been appointed, but the marginalisation of women is still prevalent. Only 17 of 124 parliamentarians are women, two of 24 ministers, four of 21 deputy ministers, 86 of 456 local councillors, none of 19 municipal chairpersons and three of 19 municipal deputy chairpersons. To address this situation, a five-year action plan is being coordinated by the MSWGCA and funded by UN agencies. The women's rights groups are currently networking with other international women's groups to build capacity to produce quality women representatives who can engage with the system to dismantle the hierarchical structures that date from before the war.

Despite these reforms, efforts are still needed to bring Sierra Leone's national legislation into line with international obligations as the legal landscape is replete with contradictory and outdated legislation that adversely affects women's access to justice, although attempts are under way to reform or repeal some of them through the Justice Sector Reform Project. Worse still, the constitution, which is the supreme law of the land, sanctions discrimination, as section 27 4 (d) (e) allows discrimination on the very issues that concern women and lead to the abuse of their rights. A notable issue is that rural women in Sierra Leone are discriminated against in marriage. Many rural women are subject to polygamous customary marriages where the husband is superior and wives are treated as property and inferior in status. Women are not allowed to inherit their deceased husbands' property under customary law, and the constitution recognises such customary law.

Even the acts that have been passed do not address all the concerns for women's protection in marriages. For example, the Devolution of Estate Act 2007, Part 1, section 1, paragraph 3 states: 'This Act Shall not apply to family property, chieftaincy property, or community property held under Customary Law', which denies the majority of rural women in Sierra Leone who are married under customary law any rights in these areas and forces them to submit to the discriminatory requirements of customary law. Worse still, section 9 (2) of the Mohammedan Act Cap 96 provides for discrimination against the wife and daughter of a Muslim who dies intestate, as only the eldest son or eldest brother or an official administrator can take out letters of administration. It should be noted that about 60 per cent of Sierra Leoneans are Muslims. These two laws therefore do next to nothing to make justice available, accessible and affordable for the majority of women when it comes to marriage, inheritance and property rights.

Women and girls are therefore disadvantaged in a patriarchal and polygamous society in accessing wealth and property they have contributed to generating and are forced into remarriage or early marriage to survive. In addition, in many parts of the country, women are debarred from holding the highest office in their communities – the paramount chieftaincy. In the last paramount chieftaincy elections, women were explicitly barred from the contest in five chiefdoms. This was challenged by women's rights activists, civil society groups and donors, but they were unable to achieve a breakthrough, as chieftaincy rites in these communities are ritualistic and exclusively managed by male-only secret societies.

Arguably, one explanation for this is that the reform processes have not been aligned with the TRC report's specific recommendations that the judiciary should not permit laws or practices to stand that are contrary to justice or which undermine the right to liberty, equality and justice. At the national level, the requirements of 30 per cent representation of women in political parties, 50/50 gender parity in representational politics and 30 per cent representation of women in the cabinet have still not been achieved, while only two out of 13 magistrates and seven out of 21 judges are women, the Family Support Unit of the Sierra Leone police is male dominated, and so on. Another explanation is that in reality the TRC lacked an enforcement mandate. There was little government ownership of the process; there were competing claims for the limited resources available; and there was a clear lack of capacity among staff on human rights and issues of sexual and gender-based violence. Furthermore, there were various frameworks for addressing the reconstruction and rehabilitation of war-torn communities, of which the TRC report was only one. These included the National Recovery Strategy, the Poverty Reduction Strategy Paper, Vision 2025, the UN Country Strategy Paper, etc, which were more highly prioritised by government and donors.

The view is now emerging, therefore, that both western and local reconciliation mechanisms should probably be used to achieve justice for voiceless victims, with the Fambul Tok[2] initiative of the Forum for Conscience increasingly gaining ground. Unlike the preliminary pact signed by the Ugandan government and rebels of the Lord's Resistance Army in June 2007[3] in which '[t]ransitional justice mechanisms, such as Mato Oput and others as practised in the communities affected by the conflict, [were to] be promoted, with necessary modifications, as a central part of the framework for accountability and reconciliation' and the advice of Kofi Annan that 'due regard must be given to indigenous and informal traditions for administering justice or settling disputes, to help them to continue their often vital role and to do so in conformity with both international standards and local traditions' (Annan 2004), there was no reference to indigenous approaches and mechanisms for seeking justice and reconciliation in Sierra Leonean communities. Although the TRC was aware of this shortcoming and used some traditional methods of reconciliation within communities, these were not enough to deliver justice to individuals through an encounter between the perpetrator and the victim leading to restoration.

Professor Allie, in his paper 'Local approaches to justice' (Allie 2009), observes that justice mechanisms are not alien to Sierra Leonean communities, as all the ethnic groups in Sierra Leone believe in the rule of law and justice as instruments for maintaining societal cohesion and harmony and have established accountability mechanisms, including prosecution, arbitration and mediation. They also abhor impunity and have developed a local justice mechanism that is community centred in character. It is partly in recognition of this fact that the processes and mechanisms for establishing the truth in local contexts are generally carried out in public, often with the active involvement of community members. This open, participatory and transparent system greatly minimises the possibility of any miscarriage of justice, and it is cheap and affordable. Thus, poor people are not denied justice because of their inability to meet the high costs of litigation found in formal, western-type courts. This opportunity was lost in rural communities where most of the sexual violence and other heinous crimes were committed and into which the perpetrators were integrated through a disarmament, demobilisation and reintegration programme that provided a lucrative package to them, including cash, skills training, educational opportunities up to university level, livelihood support that included start-up kits, agricultural inputs and seed money.

In what was considered a setback for transitional justice by many, the Lomé Agreement granted a blanket amnesty to perpetrators of sexual and gender-based violence under Article IX: 'Pardon and Amnesty', which states (emphasis added):

> To consolidate the peace and promote the cause of national reconciliation, the Government of Sierra Leone shall ensure that *no official or judicial action* is taken against any member of the RUF/SL, ex-AFRC, ex-SLA, or CDF in respect of anything done by them in pursuit of their objectives as members of those organisations, since March 1991 up to the signing of the peace agreement. In addition, legislative and other measures

necessary to guarantee immunity to former combatants, exiles and other persons, currently outside the country for reasons related to the conflict shall be adopted ensuring the full exercise of their civil and political rights, with a view to their reintegration within a framework of full legality.

Worse still, the SCSL's mandate was limited to a restrictive definition of 'those who bear the greatest responsibility', which let off many of the notorious community-level perpetrators. It also adopted a restrictive approach to the Rome Statute, providing that the SCSL may only order the forfeiture of property taken from victims by a convicted person and its return to the rightful owner. Although provision is made for victims to claim compensation against a person convicted by the SCSL, this must be done through the national courts, raising concern that the weak national justice system, coupled with the expense of such a process, will be unable to deal with these claims adequately, with dire consequences for poor and illiterate rural women.

Civil society organisations and women's rights activists such as Amnesty International, ActionAid, Campaign for Good Governance, the Women's Forum, the Forum of Conscience and the UN country team conducted campaigns and sensitisation on these issues, mobilised opinion leaders and lobbied parliamentarians to bring pressure on government to rectify these anomalies by enacting the gender and child rights bills, undertaking justice sector reforms, and accepting the TRC recommendations on the government body to implement the reparations programme and incorporating it into the pilot UNPBF.

The limitations of the special court's mandate, coupled with the lack of political will on the part of government and the misconceptions about reparations, have not only contributed to the denial of justice to victims of sexual violence in Sierra Leone, but have also delayed the implementation of the reparations programme for victims. The government deviated from the key recommendation on the agency to implement the reparations programme and went on to establish a cabinet sub-committee via a white paper in September 2005, chaired by the vice-president and headed by the attorney general, with a mandate to recommend measures to address 'some of the needs of amputees and war wounded'. This inevitably excluded all other categories, including sexual violence and child victims of the war, that were identified by the TRC. It also created a more powerful parallel structure within the political hierarchy for the implementation of the reparations programme, instead of the NaCSA, which had been recommended by the TRC as the implementing agency, based on its widely acknowledged competence and capacity to implement rehabilitation programmes.

Furthermore, the white paper was silent on the establishment of the follow-up body, the human rights commission, which was in any case not in existence by then. These two shortcomings were to have a tremendous impact on the implementation of the TRC's recommendations, as they created confusion and inertia, and there was no attempt to develop a government-led action plan to guide the implementation process. Donors also shied away from funding the reparations programme, as it symbolised guilt, and went on to fund various elements of the TRC report that would suit their agenda and were non-controversial. For instance, a World Bank mission to Sierra Leone in 2007 suggested that because of the delay in implementing the reparations programme, an alternative approach that targeted war victims under a disability project could be considered in the Children and Youth in Africa initiative, 'Supporting the Transition to Productive Lives'.[4] Consequently, there was weak dissemination of the report, poor sensitisation on key provisions and an uncoordinated implementation of the recommendations. In the event, although government and its development partners did address some of the TRC recommendations, their activities were never properly aligned with these recommendations, and normal service delivery programmes were erroneously construed as part of the reparations programme (see HRC/UNAMSIL 2007).

Unfortunately, another retributive transitional justice mechanism, as opposed to the TRC restorative justice mechanism, was set up at the same time in the form of the Special Court for Sierra Leone (SCSL), which applied a very narrow interpretation of the definition of '[t]hose who bear the greatest responsibility for serious violations of International Humanitarian Law and Sierra Leone Laws' that laid emphasis on prosecution and very little on the rehabilitation of the victims. It was disproportionately well resourced and focused on merely 13 indictees, in comparison with the TRC, which was meant to address the needs of the hundreds of thousands of severely war-affected people and the entire society with a view to building the social capital destroyed during the war. The lavish SCSL infrastructure and the millions spent on the trial and other paraphernalia contrasted with the lack of adequate support to victims. In the eyes of many of the victims, therefore, the TRC merely became an appeasement mechanism, especially as the SCSL never allowed its indictees to give open testimony at the TRC.

Under pressure from civil society, victims and the UN Mission to Sierra Leone (UNAMSIL), on 8 September 2006 NaCSA was formally designated by a vice-presidential directive as the government agency to implement a comprehensive reparations programme, and a task force was created under the chairmanship of NaCSA to advise government on the legal, institutional and financial frameworks required to implement the reparations programme within internationally acceptable standards. These tasks were fulfilled, culminating in the development of a proposal for one-year catalytic funding that was approved and funded by the UNPBF in 2008. Civil society organisations, women's rights activists and the UNAMSIL Human Rights Section were involved in the development of the programme and in designing the structures and the representation of women in them. The TRC recommendations for women were all incorporated in the design and prioritised for immediate implementation during the pilot phase, and provision was made and successfully carried out for representation by one woman and one male on the steering committee for victims and civil society groups.

However, the politicisation of the recruitment process and the lack of female representation at the decision-making level of the NaCSA – where the initial management staff of the reparations programme were all male – has further contributed to the denial of victims of sexual violence the justice, and comprehensive and effective reparations they deserve under the Rome Statute. The interface between civil society and the steering committee is weak, leading to problems in the data collection for and design and implementation of the reparations programme. For instance, many sexual and gender-based violence (SGBV) victims could not register for benefits because they were requested over the radio and in newspapers to report to NaCSA offices for registration on specific dates, which they found very difficult to do. The reparations programme is also not aligned with the wider judicial and security reform processes and civil society initiatives that are aimed at establishing mechanisms to prevent future conflict, promote good governance, strengthen institutions, address deep-seated discrimination against women, promote equality, and improve women's status and reproductive health.

The failure to align itself with these processes means that, like the other TRC recommendations, the reparations programme is being implemented as a stand-alone programme that cannot comprehensively and sustainably address the multiple issues arising out of the TRC recommendations, especially gender-based violence. Nor is it aligned with the more institutionalised and systematic community-based reconciliation programmes such as Fambul Tok, which uses local approaches to reconciliation that could afford justice to voiceless women in rural communities. For instance, Fambul Tok puts a high premium on women's participation in the structures established in communities at all levels in the reconciliation process. 'Mammy Queens' are part of the reconciliation committees, key players in the community farms in each section and heads of women's support groups in each community, and they perform a central role in traditional ceremonies with singular honour in the pouring of libations to ancestors. At an organisational level, the chief executive officer and the administrative officer of Fambul Tok are women, while others are serving as district coordinators and deputies in its operational areas.

The lack of an independent and professional assessment of victims before beneficiaries are registered means that many SGBV victims who are afraid of stigma will not be able to benefit from the scheme. For instance, an Amnesty International report in 2007 on SGBV in three out of 13 districts indicated that about 250,000 women and girls (33 per cent of the sample population) suffered from sexual violence (Amnesty International 2007), which contrasts with the current NaCSA registered figure of 2,500 for the whole country. Although provision is made in the NaCSA mandate for sexual violence war victims, this is limited to fistula surgery, while it is silent on HIV/Aids victims. Worse still, the one-off blanket compensation of about $75 for all categories of victims will not only not be enough for any viable and sustainable micro-enterprise or microcredit scheme, but also does not take into consideration the peculiar needs of female victims who were subjected to sexual violence and slavery. Most women therefore prefer to suffer in silence, unable to share their painful memories out of fear that they will be rejected by their family members and lose their future economic security. Rural woman will also be further disadvantaged by the structural imbalance within Sierra Leone's patriarchal society, as invariably the husbands or male relations will control the funds paid out to these women.

Was justice done for women?

The failure to develop an action plan to implement the TRC recommendations, which would have ensured ownership of and commitment to the TRC report, represents a major obstacle to the attainment of justice for women in Sierra Leone. The TRC recommendations devoted a whole chapter to the effect of the marginalisation of women and made concrete recommendations for women in general and women victims in particular. These are yet to be addressed in full, mainly because the Lomé Agreement and the TRC were seen more as means to achieving political ends rather than justice and restitution for women. The incorporation of a blanket amnesty clause for all perpetrators and the limitation of the SCSL mandate to try 'those who bear the greatest responsibility for serious violations of International Humanitarian Law and Sierra Leone Laws' let many notorious perpetrators off the hook. Even more repugnant was the failure to incorporate lustration for those who are known perpetrators, ostensibly because 'Sierra Leone's peace is built on the back of a negotiated settlement and lustration has the potential to be divisive and will affect national unity, peace and reconstruction of society' (TRC 2004).

The UN and civil society reacted to these blanket amnesties and have put programmes in place to address impunity in gender-based violence cases and ensure women's right to participate in the governance of their communities and the state. Coalitions of civil society groups emerged to redress this by sensitising community leaders, religious groups, and security forces and judiciary functionaries on gender-based violence, and demanding that structures be put in place, like the police's Family Support Unit, to protect women after the war and that gender issues be incorporated into the reparations programme. In particular, they called for the creation of a special gender unit within the reparations programme, which is yet to materialise, due to the all-male character of the staff. The UN, the UK Department for International Development and the European Union (EU) are all funding agencies and programmes in various parts of the country, and in its 2008 programme the EU is making provision for training and legal aid for the victims of gender-based violence.

A case in point has been the refusal to allow a prominent woman, Madame Elizabeth Toto, to contest the paramount chieftaincy elections in the highly patriarchal society of Kono in the Eastern Province, just because of her gender. Women's rights groups, the UN and civil society in general rallied to her cause and appealed against the decision in court, but she was again denied her right by the Ministry of Local Government on the specious grounds that it had decided to respect the decision of the all-male tribal authorities, who have the constitutional mandate to conduct chieftaincy elections. Attempts to pursue the cause of this woman by the UN and other women's rights groups resulted in violence that saw the hasty retreat of the delegation from all-male Kono under armed escort. This kind of approach, despite the TRC's recommendations against such discrimination against women in all spheres of life, is even more prevalent in the Northern Province, where it is unthinkable for women to aspire to contest such elections. This issue has been taken up by 50/50 and other civil society groups as a platform for advocacy for the next elections, as it has become clear that unless women are involved in community structures and traditional norms and customs are challenged, the duty bearers of the state will always concede to the patriarchy that is entrenched by tradition.

Another case in point is the degree to which women have been involved in the traditional approach of Fambul Tok at all levels, mainly because the organisation's mission and strategy is to foster reconciliation among victims and perpetrators of all ages. Unlike the reparations programme being implemented by the government, which excludes all forms of participation by the perpetrators, this approach has been able to reach out to women who were placed on the other side of the divide (i.e. in the rebels' camp) by circumstances not of their own making. Because of this, they were forced to bear the unwanted babies of combatants and, at times, to participate in the war as fighters. Their involvement with the help of Fambul Tok in community structures, projects generated by the process and traditional cleansing ceremonies has enabled them to be reconciled with both the perpetrators and their own families. John Caulker, the executive secretary of Fambul Tok, explained that his donors in the United States are so pleased with the outcome of the process that the organisation is now extending it from two districts in the east of the country to three other districts in the north, with the aim of covering the entire country.[5] One of the attributes of the approach is its involvement of the community and its partnership with local structures to ensure ownership of the process and its willingness to contribute to the process physically and materially.

Conclusion

Periods of crisis and upheaval no doubt provide opportunities for change. But they also present enormous challenges. The experience of Sierra Leone is no different. The peace process and the period of post-conflict rebuilding that followed created an opportunity to restructure the social and political order alongside infrastructural rebuilding. In reality, though, it has been difficult to transform the conditions of women. Not withstanding the attempts at various reforms, it has been difficult to shift societal norms and traditions that perpetuate women's inequality and their subjection to structural violence.

The transitional justice efforts in Sierra Leone, particularly the use of reparations, have produced marginal results at best and the results for women have been even less visible. Clearly, the TRC is not a panacea that will bring justice, accountability and restoration to victims, or promote comprehensive and sustainable reconciliation, and so a balance between western and African justice systems would be advisable for states such as Sierra Leone coming out of war. Real change towards ending violence against women requires a coordinated and sustained effort at many levels, focusing on legal and institutional reforms with particular attention paid to the repeal of all discriminatory laws and amending contradictory ones in the spirit of the TRC. The mere passing of legislation and ratification of international instruments on gender-based violence are not enough, so there should be a shift from NGOs' generic awareness programmes on human rights and women's rights to more strategic programmes that address policy issues and the operationalisation of the frameworks developed that will ensure access to justice for marginalised women.

Amnesty clauses, combined with culture, traditions and societal norms, perpetuate impunity and SGBV in Africa after conflicts. Therefore, to address SGBV adequately, reparations programme should be aligned with political, judicial and security sector reform processes in which women are represented at all levels – management, policy and operations – so that the pre-existing patriarchal structures can be dismantled. A starting point in any reparations programme is the involvement of women in the development, design and management of the programme.

There should also be a mental shift on the part of donors, who see support for reparations as acknowledgement of guilt, to a commitment to the consolidation of peace processes in countries transitioning from war to peace. It is unrealistic to expect countries like Sierra Leone coming out of devastating wars to fund reparations programmes while donors are spending huge funds on integrating perpetrators into disarmament, demobilisation and reintegration programmes and trying a few indicted individuals in special courts. Furthermore, strong political will on the part of government to ensure ownership of and commitment to the funding of a reparations programme will convince donors to support it. A coordinated approach to the implementation of TRC recommendations is also required.

Active civil society participation in the process is absolutely essential to ensure that a follow-up mechanism to the TRC report is established by law, the main provisions of the TRC report are disseminated to the populace and all the elements of a reparations programme are extended to all the categories of victims, especially women. Civil society groups are also critical in monitoring, tracking, advocating for and influencing the process, and should be supported in this regard, both financially and by the whole-hearted acceptance of their role by government.

Notes

1. The Lomé Agreement was signed between the RUF/SL and the Ahmed Tejan Kabba government in the Togolese capital of Lomé in July 1999 under the chairmanship of the then Economic Community of West African States chairperson, President Gnassimbe Eyadema of Togo. It provided the framework for a definitive settlement to the fratricidal war in Sierra Leone and reflected the desire to achieve lasting peace, national unity and reconciliation after 11 years of brutal civil war.
2. Fambul Tok is a traditional approach to reconciliation that is implemented by a local NGO known as the Forum of Conscience.
3. The LRA and the Ugandan government agreement on accountability and reconciliation which made provision for 'alternative penalties' for serious crimes or to establish 'alternative justice mechanisms'.
4. This was a 2007 World Bank initiative geared towards 'supporting the transition to productive resources' for youths and children, including the disabled.
5. Interview with John Caulker, executive director, Fambul Tok, Sierra Leone.

References

Annan, Kofi (2004) *The Rule of Law and Transitional Justice in Conflict and Post-Conflict Societies: Report to the Security Council*, S/2004/616/, http://www.undp.org/.../rule%20of%20law%20and%20transitional%20justice.pdf, accessed 17 May 2010

Allie, J.A.D. (2009) 'Local approaches to justice', paper delivered to a delegation of Ugandan officials of the Internal War Crimes Commission in the Justice, Law and Order Sector, September

Amnesty International (2007) *Sierra Leone: Getting Reparations Right for Survivors of Sexual Violence*, Freetown, Amnesty International

Lomé Peace Accord (1999) http://www.sierra-leone.org/lomeaccord.html, accessed 17 May 2010

Human Rights Commission/UN Mission to Liberia (HRC/UNAMSIL) (2007) *Report on the Consultative Conference on the Status of Implementation of The TRC Recommendations*, Freetown, HRC/UNAMSIL, November

Truth and Reconciliation Commission (TRC) (2004) *Witness to Truth: Report of the Truth and Reconciliation Commission of Sierra Leone*, Freetown, TRC

6

'Many truths were not revealed': the case of Mozambique

Helen Scanlon and Benilde Nhalevilo

I don't want to remember the past anymore. When I was kidnapped, I was 11 years old. At the base, I was chosen by one of the chiefs. I knew nothing about being a wife ... the first night that he came to fetch me, my mother cried a lot when he took me by the hand. He asked her why she was crying since I was being taken by a chief ... I never saw my mother again.

J. João, 40 years old, Beira

When many women returned, they could not cope and died; others became crazy, others returned with disabilities ... many did not manage to get husbands because the men said that that woman has been passed around by lots of men. It's not easy for us outside the city to know our rights, therefore often our lives do not progress, and we cannot look after our children.

Latifa, Homoíne

I believe that many truths were not revealed because when [my mother] tried to tell of what had happened at the bases, she found it difficult and would cry ... The family arranged for a witchdoctor to purify my mother's body as well as that of her granddaughter. They were vaccinated with a blade to introduce the medicine based on roots from the bush, so as to free them from evil spirits. Unfortunately, my mother was never totally free ... she could not cope and in the end she died.

G. Zacarias, Nampula

When the General Peace Agreement was signed in Mozambique ... the community rejected me ... Therefore I preferred to take refuge in the city [as] people did not know my story. But, as a woman, I believe that we continue to be vulnerable to other types of violence, such as domestic violence.

Anonymous, Mozambique Island

They took me together with my mother ... I had a husband who was a chief and already had five wives. Each soldier had one wife at least from among the young kidnapped women. I was lucky that I did not get pregnant. But this could have cost me my life because my husband said that I was eating at his expense and not producing anything, and that in fact I was inconveniencing him.

Aida Mulhanga, former child soldier

Mozambique's transition from over 27 years of conflict to a seemingly peaceful country has been widely lauded as an example of how local conflict resolution mechanisms can aid the journey from civil war to peace. However, as widespread violence against women in the country continues at alarming rates, questions have been increasingly asked about the legacy of the conflict for gender relations.

The arrival of the Portuguese in Mozambique in 1498 initiated their colonial rule, which lasted until 1975, when the Front for the Liberation of Mozambique (Frelimo) seized power. However, shortly after independence, the country was plunged into a brutal civil war between Frelimo and the Mozambican National Resistance (Renamo) that lasted for nearly 16 years between 1976 and 1992. This war took place in the bi-polar context of the cold war, which meant that regional and international tensions created and shaped the civil war.

The conflict resulted in the death of over a million Mozambican citizens and displaced some 40 per cent of its population. Its cost to the country's economy was estimated to be $15 billion and, according to analysts, 'resulted in every Mozambican family having at least one member or acquaintance who was killed, mutilated, or who disappeared' (Turshen 2001: 57). Analysts agree that women and children were the primary victims of the conflict, both directly and indirectly. Many women were kidnapped, raped and forcibly 'married' to combatants. They also witnessed the assassination of their husbands, siblings and children and were subject to displacement and loss of livelihood. Today, Mozambique continues to carry the economic burden of its past and was ranked as 172nd out of 177 countries in the 2007/08 United Nations (UN) *Human Development Report*.

Mozambique has undergone two transitions since independence in 1975: the first steering the transfer from colonialism to independence, and the second from civil war to democracy in 1994. Both transitions have witnessed numerous human rights violations and, as a result, different strategies have been adopted to deal with – or not – the legacy of the past.

Through gathering the narratives of a cross-section of Mozambican women, this chapter analyses some of the country's residual gender justice issues. Not only were women kidnapped, raped and forcibly 'married' to soldiers, they were also active participants in the conflict. Nonetheless, in the absence of formal justice mechanisms, those women who had been abducted or who were abused during the conflict continue to face social resettlement problems, as well as being highly vulnerable to domestic violence. This chapter evaluates the processes used in Mozambique to promote reintegration and reconciliation, with emphasis on their gendered dimensions.

Context

When Frelimo gained power in 1975 on a socialist mandate, its leaders created a one-party state, rendering all political opposition movements illegal. The government was guided by an ideology that suggested that traditional African cultural practices and organised religion restricted Mozambique's progress. From 1976 the government embarked on a policy of nationalisation, with the objective of ensuring that all property was owned by the Mozambican state. The transition was marred by political, ethnic and cultural diversity in the country. Schisms had been created during Portuguese rule when colonial infrastructure was developed primarily in the south. In contrast, the central and northern regions were under the administration of multinational companies that showed little interest in socio-economic development. Tensions were fuelled by the threat to white rule in southern Africa posed by the collapse of Portuguese control of Mozambique and Angola in 1975, which led both Rhodesia (as it was known then) and South Africa to provide clandestine logistical support, resources, funding and weapons to Renamo, Frelimo's major opponent in the civil war. In turn, the Frelimo government offered safe haven to fellow African liberation fighters from other countries, including members of the African National Congress of South Africa and the ZANU nationalists of Rhodesia (now Zimbabwe). In 1994 the Mozambican government signed the Nkomati Non-Aggression Pact with South Africa's apartheid government, which committed each country to ensuring that its territory was not used as a base for attacks against the other. However, it is widely held that South African support for Renamo continued. The collapse of the Soviet Union and the end of the apartheid regime in South Africa served to undermine external support for the war. War weariness and a devastating drought in 1991 culminated in the 1992 General Peace Agreement (GPA). The first democratic elections were held in 1994, which Frelimo won by a small majority under Joaquim Chissano, who then became president. By mid-1995 more than 1.7 million Mozambican refugees had been repatriated from neighbouring Malawi, Zimbabwe, Swaziland, Zambia, Tanzania and South Africa.

The role of Mozambican women

Following the launch of an armed struggle by Frelimo in the 1960s, many women became active participants in the liberation movement. During Frelimo's first congress in 1962, in line with the political climate of the time, there were calls for the emancipation of women. The Feminine League of Mozambique, the country's first women's organisation, was also established at this time, but it lacked a progressive mandate and focus, as its central aim was to support families. Following developments occurring among independence movements across Africa, Frelimo increasingly called for the liberation of women as part of its demands for independence. From 1966 Mozambican women participated in military training and began to embark on some security-related activities. To further women's emancipation, Frelimo's Women's Division (Destacamento Feminino) was created and, in 1973 the Mozambican Women's Organisation (Organização da Mulher Moçambicana) was formed to reach Mozambican women more broadly. Despite the rhetoric, gender roles did not undergo any transformation during the liberation struggle, as women continued to be primarily responsible for domestic tasks such as preparing food and taking care of children, while men were responsible for military activities.

During the civil war, women were participants in the conflict in a variety of ways, such as preparing food, drawing water and collecting wood. They were also deployed in attacks, were sent to steal food and were members of Renamo's Women's Division. Additionally, they were used as sexual slaves by the guerrillas, and as a result became wives and mothers. According to Elisa Muianga (1995), all women interviewed by her had landed up at bases because they had been raped by combatants, and these attacks primarily occurred when they were coming and going from their vegetable plots. Indeed, it was during the long walks that many were sexually abused, while those that resisted were generally killed. As one of her interviewees noted: 'during the walk, if the guerrillas needed a woman, they could use her ... they did not respect her disposition, nor her age' (Muianga 1995). The abduction of women to the military bases was a frequent and traumatic experience. As Latifa from Homoíne explained: 'Women suffered a lot at the bases. They worked a lot and were not given food. They had to draw water to drink and were always supervised by the soldiers to stop them from running away. They were raped and killed. It is difficult to talk about all of this again.'

While some analysts have contended that not all women at the bases were forced into relationships, interviews conducted for this chapter suggest that women had little autonomy in dictating terms of relationships. Even though there were no formal marriage ceremonies at the bases, women were assigned 'husbands'. Men in higher ranks could have more than one wife and commanders' wives enjoyed some privileges that others did not have, such as better clothing and food. According to Muianga, although fights between women for the same husband were prohibited, these did sometimes occur due to the competition for resources:

> Those women who had been kidnapped and taken as wives faced the risk of pregnancy and the danger of having a child at the base from which we had to run away. The others were running away with babies on their shoulders. And those babies that

cried a lot were killed so that they would not to make a noise and reveal the hiding place to the enemy. (Muianga 1995)

Furthermore, in certain areas women faced suspicions regarding pregnancy. According to Florência Notisso, from the district of Inharrime in Inhambane, her daughter had been kidnapped and was taken as a wife by a commander. However, she notes that in that region the following happened if a woman fell pregnant:

They had to kill her, if not, the one who had impregnated her or the baby itself would certainly die. Thus during her entire pregnancy they threatened her. Luckily for her, the baby was still-born. As soon as that happened she had a traditional treatment so that she would no longer get pregnant again. When the war ended, she ran away immediately and returned home. Today she is married to another man, but because of that treatment, she can no longer have children. She is still traumatised.

Filomena Alfiado from Inharrime noted how when they encountered soldiers: 'they cut off the penises of men and boys. They cut off the lips of us girls and the adult women ... Today all I want to do is to be able to study and work and I would like my lips to be restored.' Similarly, a woman from Nampula revealed:

My mother was 47 years old, she was physically and sexually assaulted by soldiers, very often when her granddaughter was nearby. Once, according to her, she was raped when she had malaria. When she tried to resist, they opened a grave, threatening her with death. Then they ordered her to grind chillies, which they put in her vagina.

Although the conflict had had a major impact on women, the GPA did not make any allusion to gender issues, neither in terms of its structure nor its contents. It is worth noting that none of the delegates during the Rome negotiations was a woman. According to Raul Domingos, the head of the negotiation team representing Renamo, 'at that stage, most of us were not aware of gender issues ... but if the Agreement were made today, women would have to be heard as direct participants ... we have to include women in the process'. In turn, Dom Diniz Sengulane, who also participated in the peace process, noted: 'we made a huge mistake because the great peace commissions only consisted of men ... and yet men were the ones that made war. Those who went around abducting and killing women and children were men ... therefore, I do not believe that men alone can bring complete peace.'

Addressing Mozambique's transition

Mozambique's independence struggle was marred by disappearance and assassination of those who opposed Portuguese rule, as well as those opposed to Frelimo. Some Frelimo leaders in the liberation struggle were, in turn, excluded from the new government, generating further discontent, both among those who had remained in the country during the conflict and those who returned to the country from exile. Traditional leaders – both chiefs and traditional healers – were also excluded from political life, despite their community leadership roles. They therefore had little incentive to embrace the new government. This, together with the prevailing sense of alienation in the rural areas in the centre and north of the country, made civil war almost inevitable.

Following independence, the government, led by Samora Machel, established an initiative to seek out those *comprometidos* (the compromised) who had collaborated with the Portuguese. Between 1978 and 1982 a number of re-education camps were established 'to transform the compromised based on the presumption of guilt, repentance, punishment and re-education' (Igreja and Dias-Lambranca, 2008: 64). At this time many Mozambican families were also forced to leave the country due to their support of the colonial regime. Repressive legislation was also implemented such as the reinstitution of the death penalty in March 1979 and the reintroduction of the colonial practice of whipping in 1983. Both laws were approved by parliament retroactively, following a series of public executions and whippings.

Frelimo's re-education camps had a profound impact on many families and their implications are still felt today. Parents and children, and husbands and wives, were separated permanently and the effect on those women left behind has not been addressed. While some of those in Frelimo acknowledge that the re-education camps were problematic, others have justified them as 'a necessary evil'. Complaints by those directly affected were not presented in an organised or structured manner, largely due to the lack of proper platforms through which families could direct complaints. The political climate also created obstacles for those seeking to challenge the regime. As a result, the truth regarding numerous assassinations and disappearances is still questioned by Mozambicans.

During both of Mozambique's transitions, the possibility of prosecutions for crimes committed during the country's conflict were ruled out, most significantly through the 1992 peace agreement. The GPA, with the support of security forces, government and opposition leaders, specifically eliminated the possibility of prosecutions and no formal transitional justice mechanisms were instituted. Instead, the first democratically elected government of Mozambique instituted a policy of reconciliation between the former warring groups. Responsibility for atrocities committed during the conflict was never discussed and as a result the majority of victims were neither identified nor compensated. Furthermore, numerous questions remain over the truth regarding assassinations, disappearances and abuses committed during the conflict. The focus was placed squarely on peace instead of justice and as a result a significant role was played by faith and traditional communities in steering reintegration and reconciliation. The amnesty embedded in the 1992 peace agreement resulted in a national discourse of 'forgive and forget', which is now compounded by reticence about revisiting the wounds of the past. Even if the political will to pursue prosecutions were to emerge, Mozambique currently lacks the investigative and judicial resources to do so. As a result, major systemic sources of conflict were left unresolved. This has led analysts to argue that the country suffers from collective amnesia. But it is also argued that the involvement of external forces made criminal justice against perpetrators complicated. For example, political analyst Irae Baptista Lundin commented: 'Who ought we to have prosecuted? If not the Rhodesians, South Africans and other international players, why Renamo and Frelimo?'

Disarmament, demobilisation and reintegration

Mozambique's formal disarmament, demobilisation and reintegration (DDR) process was led by the United Nations Operations in Mozambique (ONUMOZ), which had been created in October 1992 under Security Council Resolution 797. While the DDR process did try to tackle economic and social reintegration, it did little to address the psycho-social rehabilitation of ex-combatants or their victims. It also failed to address gender during demobilisation and the subsequent creation of the new Armed Forces for the Defence of Mozambique, despite the fact that women had been part of both government and Renamo forces during the conflict. According to Jacinta Jorge from the Association for Peace Promotion, herself a former combatant, the reintegration kits distributed by ONUMOZ only included men's clothes, shoes and underwear.

A further failure by ONUMOZ related to social resettlement schemes, whose activities for women focused on their reproductive or domestic roles, for example the provision of sewing schemes. The result of this has been that former women soldiers have not benefited from the same opportunities and rights as their former male colleagues. The Association of Demobilised Women Soldiers, composed of former Frelimo and Renamo soldiers, was therefore created to advocate for the rights of female ex-combatants. The association has tried to support the resettlement of former female soldiers from both sides of the conflict and to support the improvement of their social condition and status.

The UN High Commissioner for Refugees (UNHCR) worked with a number of local non-governmental organisations (NGOs), including the Red Cross of Mozambique and the Christian Council of Mozambique, in the transporting of 1.7 million returnees and their reintegration. Despite the duration and brutality of the Mozambican conflict, as well as concern over the sustainability of the peace agreement, refugees were keen to return home. The peak of resettlement took place in 1994, with the return of 804,376 people in total, but unfortunately these figures were not disaggregated for gender.

In 1994 UNHCR also carried out about 500 community rehabilitation projects aimed at restoring essential services in sectors such as health and education, improving the availability of potable water, and making remote regions more accessible through the construction and repair of roads and bridges. The Mozambican reintegration programme gave a high priority to the distribution of agricultural implements to returnees and displaced people, demobilised soldiers and other needy groups.

However, there were no specific programmes aimed at women's reintegration, as had occurred with former child soldiers. A 1994 study by the UN Children's Fund in the central and southern zones of the country noted that women were disproportionately affected by the conflict in psychological, physical and sexual ways (UNICEF 1994).

The report's conclusions are backed by Muianga's study on the impact of the war on women in Mandlakazi, in which she argues that the process of the reintegration of women requires specific considerations (Muianga 1995). For example, a married woman's resettlement did not solely depend on her family and community, but also on her husband's family. Muianga notes that in Mandlakazi in the southern zone, when women returned, they would go to their own relatives' houses. The family members of married women were responsible for informing their husband's family. If the husband's family were prepared to accept her, the woman was returned to her husband's home.

However, those women taken as 'wives' during the conflict were not considered to be married by their communities, particularly because traditional marriage rituals had not been observed, notably the *lobola* (bride wealth) that would have been due to her family. These women faced specific challenges over reintegration, as interviewee Alda Mulhanga explained regarding her own experience: 'Today I have three children but I am not married. When these men get involved with a woman like me, who was a child soldier and a woman forced to be the wife of a military chief, it is only to take advantage of us. Therefore it is difficult for us to get married.'

Single women interviewed for this study in the districts of Massinga and Homoíne also note the difficulties for bush wives in reintegrating:

In the beginning, they said that they accepted us. But with the passing of time, men only used us and when they meet someone who has not gone through our situation, they leave us ... Sometimes we try to hide the fact that we belonged to other men in the war. But many saw us there at the bases when we were the wives of other men. Therefore we stay alone.

Those who returned without children were more successful in beginning a new life than those who had returned with children. In Mozambique, marriage is important for women, since, beyond social recognition, it provides them with access to land and other possessions.

In some cases, married women returning after they had been abducted found that their husbands had acquired other wives in their absence. Traditionally, in the case of polygamous marriages, the first wife has special rights compared to the wives taken after her, such as a better house, the right to involvement in decision making regarding property or family life, and a lower domestic load. However, those returnees who found their husband married to another woman also discovered that their status as first wife depended on the wishes and decision of the husband and his family.

Nonetheless, there are many examples of women who had been abducted or who were soldiers during the conflict being reintegrated into their communities through traditional rituals conducted by healers and religious leaders. The objective of these purification rituals was to 'wash' the woman clean of her past and as a result give her 'new' life. These rituals consisted of various phases, including announcing to the ancestors that the person had recently returned from war and was asking for their forgiveness for any violent acts they may have perpetrated. Many women went through these rituals and were incorporated into their own and their husbands' families. Among the women's narratives gathered by Muianga, up to 90 per cent of interviewees reported that they had undergone traditional purification rituals.

As a further example, Adelina from Nampula Province told us that she returned home in 1992 after the GPA:

I came alone with my son aged 12 years. When I arrived, people started to cry because they thought that I had died. I was very thin. I never told of all that had happened to me during the war because it is difficult for me to talk about the horrible things that had happened to me. I was treated by a traditional healer of the area, who washed me to take away all the bad spirits I was bringing. I bathed in bush roots and they vaccinated me with a blade to put the medicine in my body for my own protection and to remove the bad luck I was bringing.

Purification rites undoubtedly contributed towards reconciliation in Mozambique, and one of the factors that contributed to forgiveness was the understanding that many combatants were unwillingly involved in acts of violence, which was particularly relevant for those women who had been abducted and were forced to become combatants. However, there is widespread criticism of traditional mechanisms for their failure to address basic rights. More critically, many have questioned their ability to promote justice and reconciliation.

Furthermore, for those women who had been victims of the conflict, the process of social reintegration did not provide space for their experiences to be heard. As Latifa, from Homoíne, noted: 'It was dangerous to talk about everything that happened during the war. The community can take advantage; it's better to keep quiet … It's difficult to go back and talk about all of this.' Many women rejected by their communities were forced to take refuge in the urban areas. An anonymous woman from Mozambique Island noted that:

when the General Peace Agreement was signed, I was released in 1992 and returned to Mozambique Island to be together with my family members. My parents received me, but the community rejected me, I felt this through their looks and comments, because they knew that I had belonged to other men during the war. Therefore I preferred to take refuge in Nampula. The city is big and people don't know my background.

As already noted, the majority of Mozambican women only have access to resources through their fathers or through marriage, which meant that economic reintegration was closely tied to social reintegration. Thus, during Mozambique's transition, one of the biggest concerns for women was over securing access to land and water. Many feared that they would be unable to recover their land that had been occupied during the conflict and, if they did manage to reclaim their abandoned and drought-stricken vegetable plots, that these would no longer be productive. Traditionally, under patrilineal societies in the south, although it was a woman's responsibility to work the land, in the event of a divorce she would have to go back to her birth family's land. Even in the largely matrilineal north, following a divorce the land would become the property of the woman's male relatives. Following the conflict, the 1997 Land Act provides one of the most gender-friendly land laws in the region through its combination of formal and customary law. While land continues to be controlled by the state, the law removes the need for written evidence during any land dispute, which is critical in a country where over 70 per cent of women are illiterate. Further changes included provision that land occupied for over ten years could legally be cultivated. The act also included a clause securing women's property rights. At the economic level, some discriminatory laws were revoked, including those granting only men access to finance and denying women credit without the consent of their husbands. The creating of small loans for women formed part of post-conflict gender reforms aimed at improving women's economic and social situation.

Women's achievements during Mozambique's transition have included a significant increase in the number of women in decision-making bodies, as women make up 34.8 per cent of parliamentarians. As already noted, steps have also been taken to ensure greater gender equality through legislative acts such as the Land Act, the 2004 Family Act and the 2009 Domestic Violence Act. However, there are still major obstacles to women realising their rights, particularly in rural areas. These include women's lack of knowledge of their rights; the lack of mechanisms to ensure the enforcement of the law; and the pressure of traditional and cultural practices that contradict these rights. All of this is aggravated by the fact that law enforcement remains influenced by customary law. Furthermore, a culture of impunity surrounds gender-based violations, resulting in perpetrators not being penalised, and very often women are revictimised.

The lack of implementation of women's rights mechanisms is clear. Domestic violence against women, particularly spousal rape (which is not against the law), remains endemic. Despite the passage of the 2009 Domestic Violence Act, it is still generally accepted that a man can beat his wife, while cultural pressure discourages women from pursuing legal accountability. In many cases of rape, families choose to offer financial compensation or marriage to the victim. According to a 2006 survey, over 50 per cent of women had suffered an act of physical or sexual violence by a man at some point in their lives, 37 per cent in the previous five years, and 21 per cent during the previous year.

Of the more than 1.5 million people infected by HIV and Aids in the country, over 60 per cent are women, and they face specific challenges. A local NGO, Kukuyana, has recorded numerous cases of women being forced to leave their homes when their status is discovered. The organisation has also noted that where women were widowed by Aids, they were often accused of being witches by their communities. Furthermore, challenges women face in accessing economic and social rights are aggravated by a lack of access to education. The rate of illiteracy among urban women continues to be more than 50 per cent, while in rural areas 81.2 per cent of women are illiterate. This has a direct influence on the continued weak political participation of women, particularly in the rural areas, as well as the failure of women to access various resources, including finances. Social issues related to women's and girls' disproportionately high workload and sexual abuse are causes of the high level of girls dropping out of the education system.

The way forward

Mozambique's peaceful transition came at the expense of ensuring accountability for the wide-scale gender-based human rights violations that took place during the civil war. By analysing women's narratives, it becomes clear that their notions of peace are closely linked to gender equality and ensuring that Mozambique's culture of impunity is challenged. Given the length of the conflict and Mozambique's continued economic challenges, victims noted that gender justice needs to centre on improving their current circumstances. Access to education, land and justice, particularly in the resolution of domestic conflicts, constitutes some of the current priorities identified by women. Nonetheless, many of the inequalities faced by women today have their roots in the conflict, and the continuum of violence against women in modern-day Mozambique needs to be recognised. One of the key challenges facing the country stems from impunity for gender-based crimes and thus efforts are needed to strengthen legal and judicial mechanisms in order to transform gender-sensitive jurisprudence into tangible benefits for those women who need it.

Bibliography

Cobban, H. (2006) *Amnesty after Atrocity?: Healing Nations after Genocide and War Crimes*, Boulder, Paradigm Publishers

Igreja, V., Dias-Lambranca, B. and Richters, A. (2008) 'Gamba spirits, gender relations and healing in post-civil war Gorongosa, Mozambique', *Journal of the Royal Anthropological Institute*, vol. 14, no. 2, pp. 353–71

Igreja, V. (2008) 'Memories as weapons: the politics of peace and silence in post-civil war Mozambique', *Journal of Southern African Studies*, vol. 34, no. 3, pp. 539–56

Minow, M. (1998) *Between Vengeance and Forgiveness: Facing History after Genocide and Mass Violence*, Boston, Beacon Press

Muianga, E. (1995) 'Women and war: the reintegration of female returnees from the Renamo bases in Mandlakazi (Gaza province, South of the country)' ('Mulheres e Guerra: Reintegração Social das Mulheres Regressadas das Zonas da Renamo no distrito de Mandlakazi, província de Gaza (sul do país)', unpublished PhD dissertation, University Eduardo Mondlane, Mozambique

Turshen, Meredeth (2001) 'The political economy of rape: an analysis of systematic rape and sexual abuse during armed conflict in Africa', in Moser, C. and Clark, F. (eds) *Victims, Perpetrators or Actors: Gender Armed Conflict and Political Violence*, Zed Books, London

United Nations Children's Fund (UNICEF) (1990) *National Situational Analysis of Children and Women*, Mozambique, UNICEF

United Nations Children's Fund (UNICEF) (1994) *The Situation of Women and Children in Mozambique*, Maputo, UNICEF

Part 3
Regional organisations

7

ECOWAS, women and security

Eka Ikpe

In this chapter I interrogate the place of women in the security sector governance approaches and structures that have been developed by the Economic Community of West African States (ECOWAS). In particular I chart the influence of the changing global security context on Africa since the end of the cold war. In doing this, I question the engagement (or lack thereof) with the concerns of women in the development of a peace and security agenda in the sub-region. This debate is of particular pertinence, given ECOWAS's vision at the end of the first decade of the 21st century of an organisation of peoples rather than just member states.

In examining the participation of women in security governance in West Africa, I focus primarily on the set of normative frameworks that have become part of the ECOWAS peace and security architecture. I particularly examine the roles, responsibilities and rights that are afforded to women in these instruments and the basis upon which this is done.

The chapter is divided into three parts. First I investigate how the debate around issues of security governance emerged in the development of the ECOWAS peace and security processes. In this discussion, I am especially cognisant of the contextual realities that gave rise to these developments. There is an initial reference to the global security environment at the end of the cold war and the emergent ECOWAS peace and security architecture, as well as a consideration of the definitive impact of the engagement of ECOWAS in the civil conflict in Liberia. In this section I also consider how women's concerns have featured within the ECOWAS peace and security architecture.

The second part interrogates the extent of women's engagement in the ECOWAS peace and security architecture, and reviews the workings of the ECOWAS conflict prevention system in two stages. First, I analyse the principal tool that has been developed to actualise the engagement of women in peace and security in the ECOWAS Conflict Prevention Framework (ECPF). Second, I examine the empirical space of the ECOWAS Commission itself to understand the extent to which the ECPF is implemented, and I study the participation of women in peace and security structures, particularly in senior decision-making positions. The central objective of this section is to examine how attempts at transforming approaches to security, and in particular conflict prevention, engage with women as key players.

The final and concluding part presents what is instructive about the development of the ECOWAS peace and security processes, as illustrated by the discussions in preceding sections. There is particular reference to its engagement with the role of women in peace and security structures. What lessons can be learnt, and what are the shortcomings that can be addressed?

Security of the state, the people, and then women

ECOWAS has been lauded as being exemplary in its institutional engagement with the violent conflicts that beset the West African region through the 1980s, 1990s and to a lesser extent through the first decade of the 21st century, in Liberia, Sierra Leone, Côte d'Ivoire and Guinea Bissau. Its approach has centred on a needs-based process that came into existence as result of a succession of violent conflicts in West Africa. Its engagement with women in developing a peace and security system has followed a long trajectory; this included, among other things, how understanding of the notion of security expanded from a focus on the state to engagement with citizens. This section charts the shared trajectory of the evolving notion of security and the implications for women and for the peace and security agenda in the West African region.

Between sovereignty and evolving notions of security

ECOWAS, which was established in 1975, was to be the sole economic community in the West Africa region with 'the purpose of integration and the realisation of the objectives of the African Economic Community' (ECOWAS 1975). Concerns about security chiefly featured as a principle of participation in the economic community or in the context of food security (ECOWAS 1975, Articles 4 and 25). However, even at this stage, structures were proposed to ensure the maintenance of the principle of security within the treaty. With regard to the management of violent conflicts, there were the provisions for the peaceful settlement of disputes as well as for regional peace and security observation systems and peacekeeping forces (ECOWAS 1975, Article 58).

The treaty had much to say about the role of women in relation to the ECOWAS goal of regional integration. Article 63, entitled 'Women and Development', detailed tasks for member states and for the ECOWAS Commission to ensure 'the enhancement of the economic, social and cultural conditions of women' in the sub-region (ECOWAS 1975, Article 63). There was also a call for support for women and women's organisations alongside other constituencies within the sub-region (ECOWAS 1975, Articles 3, 61 and 82).

In the immediate aftermath of the establishment of ECOWAS there were a series of efforts to strengthen the provisions for addressing security threats in West Africa. During the initial phase of these efforts (until at least 1991), the broader West African citizenry hardly featured within these provisions.

ECOWAS's explicit concern with peace and security was taken a step further with the establishment of the ECOWAS Protocol on Non-Aggression in 1978. The protocol's preamble included the following: 'Considering that the Economic Community of West African States ... cannot attain its objectives save in an atmosphere of peace and harmonious understanding among the member states of the community...' (ECOWAS 1978). This was prompted by events in West Africa at that time that could be perceived as threatening 'the purpose of integration and the realisation of the objectives of the African Economic Community'. Mercenaries had, for example, attacked Benin in 1977 and there was a major coup d'état in Ghana in 1981 (Olonisakin and Levitt 1999).

An additional point of interest was the protocol's invocation of the conflict prevention provisions within the UN charter. This included a call to refrain from the threat or use of force against independent states (ECOWAS 1978, Article 2). Similarly, the provision in the Organisation of African Unity (OAU) charter on the territorial integrity and sovereignty of all states was a bedrock of the protocol (ECOWAS 1978, Article 1). The UN system provided the foundation for policy on the prevention of violent conflict, with the OAU provisions reinforcing the need to respect the sovereignty of independent states. This more vigorous approach to regional security indicates the significance that was attached to peace as a precondition for economic integration and development. The reliance on the UN charter and the provisions of the OAU was a way of validating the budding ECOWAS security infrastructure and linking it to the global security system.

The Protocol on Non-Aggression was considered to be lacking bite as there was no mechanism for enforcement. In particular, it was criticised for not providing the means for an institutionalised response in case of its breach (Kabia 2009: 67). The drive to strengthen the call for non-aggression was encouraged by the emergence of the Mutual Assistance in Defence Protocol (ECOWAS 1981). This protocol also referenced the international security system of the UN and the supremacy of state sovereignty as outlined in the OAU charter. The principal objective of this protocol was to affirm the understanding that armed aggression or threats to a member state affected the community as a whole; member states were to resolve to support one another militarily in such circumstances. The major conceptual addition of these instruments to the ECOWAS security system was the introduction of internal security threats and the provision of a forum to discuss this.[1] These additions merely underscored ECOWAS's preoccupation with state sovereignty. This preoccupation with the security of independent and sovereign states did not necessarily address the challenge posed by intra-state conflicts.

These efforts were intended to enable ECOWAS to take a comprehensive approach to building a community by ensuring a peaceful environment within which to pursue the largely economic objectives of regional integration. It was, however, within this realm of regional economic integration that limitations on the role of women remained. Peace and security were very much the activities of defence forces and the military, as was evident in the institutions that emerged from the Protocol Relating to Mutual Assistance on Defence, including the Authority, the Defence Council and the Defence Commission (ECOWAS 1981, Article 3). Civilians, and especially women, were given little recognition as security actors. This was largely a result of the dominance of authoritarian and military regimes in West Africa during this period. This resulted in what has been aptly described as 'a long period of exclusion of civilians from security discourse under authoritarian rule' (Olonisakin 2009).

The most critical challenge to the efficacy of the ECOWAS instruments for addressing peace and security within the community was the narrow interpretation of 'security', which applied exclusively to the state. This focus on national security and the preservation of the sovereignty of nation states may have been justified in the immediate post-independent era, following a series of hard-won independence struggles. As a result at the establishment of ECOWAS, regional (in)security in West Africa was seen from the perspective of inter-state (between states) violence. This was reflected in the fundamental principles of the Treaty of Lagos, namely, non-aggression between member states; maintenance of regional peace; stability and security through the promotion and strengthening of good neighbourliness; and peaceful settlement of disputes among member states (ECOWAS 1975, Article 4). The onset of large-scale intra-state (within a state) armed conflict would later alter this state-focused perspective on regional security.

Relating governance to security of peoples

The eruption of violent conflict in the West African region after the establishment of the instruments noted above called the efficacy of the ECOWAS security arrangements into question. It became clear that the focus on inter-state conflict at the expense of intra-state conflict (based on the principle of state sovereignty) was ineffective for maintaining peace in the sub-region. The conflicts inadvertently put the security needs of the broader citizenry in the spotlight. The particular challenges faced by women in these conflicts, particularly physical and sexual abuse and torture, eventually gained attention. Given that it was impossible to realise the central objective of economic integration in the sub-region in a context of intra-state conflict, from 1990 onwards ECOWAS was forced to intervene in Liberia, Sierra Leone, Guinea Bissau and Côte d'Ivoire.

In this chapter I focus on the Liberian conflict, given its impact on the development of the ECOWAS peace and security architecture. The Liberian conflict demonstrated the need for a re-examination of ECOWAS's preoccupation with state sovereignty and the implications of this for intervening in internal conflicts. This conflict also tested ECOWAS's capacity to respond to an outbreak of violent conflict, especially given that the immediate post-cold war era was characterised by limited international interest in Africa and the onset of 'Afro-fatigue' (Adeniji 1997).

The Liberian crisis compelled a reassessment of the ECOWAS security mechanism in the wake of broader conceptual developments in the notion of security. The result was a revised institutional approach, which linked intra-state conflict and regional peace and security. This was reinforced with the establishment of the ECOWAS Declaration of Political Principles in 1991, which recognised the relationship between governance and peace and security. Alongside the continued dedication to maintaining peace and security in the sub-region, ECOWAS was committed to the promotion of democratic governance systems, based on the rights of citizens to participate in democratic processes (ECOWAS 1991, paragraph 6).

It is important to note that this emphasis on democracy was also influenced by a broader regional shift at the end of the cold war towards reforming systems of political governance. Following the drive in the 1970s and 1980s for economic liberalism, in the 1990s the political sphere came under increasing pressure to liberalise systems of governance. Keller (1996) pointed to the trend towards democratic governance in Africa and alluded to their dependence on the preceding era's economic liberalisation. In addition, the late 1990s also saw the emergence of the at times contested notion of human security: this situated security at the level of the individual while promoting a multifaceted notion of security that included economic, political and physical security.

The Declaration of Political Principles therefore signified an evolving understanding of security within ECOWAS. The document made the first explicit reference to the need to ensure the security and rights of ECOWAS citizens on an individual basis (ECOWAS 1991, paragraph 5). As before, reference was made in the introduction to the African Charter on Human and People's Rights and to international instruments which set out to uphold human rights. This highlighted the efforts being made to ensure that ECOWAS's instruments were consistent with international and, especially, continental instruments. There was no explicit mention of women and the document was replete with the sole use of male pronouns. However, there was the stated commitment to respect and ensure the enjoyment of human rights for all West African citizens without exception. This was important as it reinforced a break with the exclusive focus on state security.

Against the background of changing approaches to governance systems, ECOWAS was compelled to address the outbreak of violent conflict in Liberia. At the start of the conflict in 1989, the UN and the OAU did not take any collective action to address the deteriorating situation (Ero 1995). With no real support from outside the region, ECOWAS was forced to intervene to try to stem the crisis in Liberia. As a result of the unfolding drama in Liberia, at the 13th summit of the heads of state of the ECOWAS countries, a five-member standing mediation committee was asked to formulate proposals for a peaceful settlement to the Liberian civil war (Ero 1995).

This committee later called for a peacekeeping force in Liberia (Ero 1995). This resulted in the deployment of the Economic Community of West African States Ceasefire Monitoring Group (ECOMOG) forces in Liberia on 25 August 1990 (Ero 1995). This ECOMOG deployment was pivotal to the engagement of ECOWAS in resolving violent conflict in West Africa and therefore to its overall security architecture. Following this first deployment in 1990, ECOWAS was embroiled in the Liberia conflict for a period of 14 years in total. The first war ended with elections in 1997, which Charles Taylor won by a landslide. A second crisis began in 1999 with armed opposition to Taylor's government. The resulting exile of Taylor in Nigeria and the signing of a Comprehensive Peace Agreement (CPA) in Ghana in

2003 resulted in the deployment of a second regional force, the ECOWAS Mission in Liberia (ECOMIL); this was responsible for security in Liberia until it handed over to a UN force.

The crucial deployment of ECOMOG troops to Liberia signified a doctrinal shift in the understanding of security as going beyond the state to include the security of people. The objective of the peacekeeping troops was to 'keep peace, restore law and order and ensure that a cease-fire agreed to by the warring factions in Liberia was respected' (UN 1993). Attempts to fulfil this mandate forced some understanding of the particular security needs faced by the population of Liberia in this conflict. Women in particular were badly affected.

General Festus Okonkwo[2] reported on the security threats to men and women during the conflict, as observed by ECOMOG. He noted that while men suffered brutal deaths and occasionally the humiliation of barbaric amputations, women were among the worst affected in the violence against the civilian population. The ordeals that were inflicted on them included brutal deaths, marathon rapes, abductions and forced marriages (Okonkwo 2008). It was noted that some female fighters were reportedly abducted and forcibly recruited as combatants, while other women who had been raped joined as a form of protection (Okonkwo 2008). A particularly difficult challenge facing ECOMOG was the incidence of sexual violence against women perpetrated by ECOMOG personnel themselves. It has been reported that ECOMOG soldiers would coerce sex workers into compliance, including in some cases children as young as eight years of age (Cain 1999).

Some of the realities of the impact of conflict on women's security were clearly reflected in the peace and security architecture of ECOWAS, in particular in one of its most influential instruments to date, the Protocol Relating to the Mechanism for Conflict Prevention, Resolution, Peacekeeping and Security (also known as 'the mechanism'). The mechanism effectively replaced the preceding Protocols on Non-Aggression and Mutual Assistance in Defence with its endorsement by the heads of state in August 1999. In its introduction it stated that it was 'convinced of the need to develop effective policies that will alleviate the suffering of the civil population, especially women and children, and restore life to normalcy after conflicts or natural disasters, and desirous

131

of making further efforts in the humanitarian sphere' (ECOWAS 1999). This was a clear statement of support and recognition of the need for women to play a role in peace and security matters. These roles included mediation, conciliation and facilitation, and support for women as a vulnerable group in the peace-building process (ECOWAS 1999, Articles 20, 40 and 44).

The ECOWAS mechanism reinforced the existing notion of the security of the state alongside that of the individual. It emphasised the principle that the security of the state and the individual were inextricably linked and emphasised the need to protect fundamental human rights and international humanitarian laws (ECOWAS 1999, Article 2). This was backed by a provision for intervention in internal conflicts and where human rights were violated (ECOWAS 1999, Article 25). The mechanism also demonstrated the significance of governance systems as a basis for security in the development of peace and security instruments. In its introduction, the document referred to the vital importance of 'good governance, the rule of law and sustainable development for peace and conflict prevention' in the sub-region (ECOWAS 1999).

An important first in ECOWAS's security apparatus was that the mechanism also began the formalisation of conflict prevention by including in its definition of member states in crisis 'a Member State facing serious and persisting problems or situations of extreme tension which, if left unchecked, could lead to serious humanitarian disaster or threaten peace and security in the sub-region' (ECOWAS 1999, Articles 20, 40 and 44). This was a considerable distance from the initial position that state sovereignty took priority over all other considerations.

The introduction in 2001 of the Protocol on Democracy and Good Governance as a supplementary protocol to the mechanism saw the deepening of requirements of member state governments to include separation of powers, strengthened parliaments and independent judiciaries (ECOWAS 2001, Article 1). It also targeted the means of transfer of power in member states by insisting that elections must be free and fair, and that any changes to systems of governance must be constitutional (ECOWAS 2001, Article 1).

The aim of the supplementary protocol was to set out norms and standards for democratic governance in the sub-region, with an emphasis on electoral processes and the rule of law in relation to governance systems. Emphasis on the citizenry was reinforced by references to popular decision making and the protection of rights as set out in continental and international human rights instruments. Particular reference was made to women's rights (ECOWAS 2001, Article 2). With the recognition that governance was foundational to security, the document also highlighted the importance of women as a necessary party to democratic systems by including provisions asserting the rights of men and women to equal participation in democratic processes and the elimination of all forms of discrimination against women (ECOWAS 2001, Articles 2 and 40). Furthermore, the capacity of women to effectively participate was addressed in the requirement for improved access to education for women (ECOWAS 2001, Article 30).

It is necessary to acknowledge that this increased recognition of the impact of conflict on women, and the call for a greater role for women in peace and security processes embedded in the ECOWAS peace and security architecture was also driven by actors outside ECOWAS. Input from civil society on the mainstreaming of gender issues with regard to peace and security only dates from the early 2000s, but has had a significant effect. The Women in Peacebuilding Network (WIPNET), part of the West Africa Network for Peace, was created in 2001 with the focus on promoting the participation of women in policy formulation and the implementation of peace and security (Ebo, forthcoming). WIPNET has played an active role in attempts to mainstream gender issues within the ECOWAS framework. In 2004 the network hosted a meeting of women's groups and the ECOWAS Gender Unit to develop a policy framework for mainstreaming women's issues in peace and security in West Africa, and it has followed up on this (Ebo, forthcoming).

The women's peace and security agenda in West Africa has also been heavily supported by women activists. Particularly visible is the Mano River Women's Peace Network (MARWOPNET), which has responded to the impact of armed conflict in the Mano River Union (Olonisakin 2009). The West Africa Civil Society Forum (WACSOF) has also been active in gender mainstreaming, for example in their work advocating for the implementation of UN Security Council Resolution 1325 at the 2006 ECOWAS council of ministers' meeting in Ouagadougou, Burkina Faso (Ebo, forthcoming).

Notably, the engagement of ECOWAS with civil society mirrored the long trajectory in transforming the understanding of security issues to emphasise human security as well as state security. Although civil society actors were active on peace and security issues in local and national contexts, prior to 2000 there was limited engagement with ECOWAS (Olonisakin 2009). In fact, it was not until 2003 that the WACSOF was created as a forum for West African civil society engagement with ECOWAS (Ebo, forthcoming). This has also been driven from within as the ECOWAS leadership, immediate past-President Ibn Chambas[3] and the former deputy executive secretary, the late General Chiekh Oumar Diarra, were keenly engaged in identifying analysts, policy practitioners and activists on security and development issues in the sub-region (Olonisakin 2009). The extent to which the ECOWAS Commission broadened this engagement to highlight the inclusion of women in ECOWAS peace and security processes is the focus of the next section.

The ECPF and the ECOWAS Commission

The development of the ECOWAS security system is the story of a broadening of focus from a sole emphasis on regional integration to (eventually) an emphasis on peace and security in West Africa. Its understanding of security issues has extended from a concern with state security to include security of the individual. With this has come the increasing need to be cognisant of the impact of conflict on women as well as their need to participate in peace and security processes. In this section I examine the extent to which it has been possible to fully incorporate women into the ECOWAS peace and security architecture by examining the ECOWAS Conflict Prevention Framework (ECPF). I also examine the ECOWAS Commission by reviewing the roles that women play in a senior decision-making capacity.

Engaging women in peace and security

The ECPF is seen as supplying 'a reference for the ECOWAS system and member states in their efforts to strengthen human security in the sub-region' (ECOWAS 2008: paragraph 5). In this document, 'human security' is defined as the creation of conditions to eliminate pervasive threats to people's human rights, livelihood, safety and life; the protection of human and democratic rights and the promotion of human development to ensure freedom from fear and freedom from want (ECOWAS 2008: paragraph 6). Conflict prevention is broadly defined to include addressing imminent conflict threats through early warning and preventive disarmament and deployment as well by addressing structural issues. It includes the development of longer-term strategies such as peace building and institutional and developmental reforms (ECOWAS 2008).

The ECPF comprises components that tackle pivotal issues for conflict prevention in the West African sub-region. These are early warning; preventive diplomacy; democracy and political governance; human rights and the rule of law; media; natural resource governance; cross-border initiatives; security governance; practical disarmament; women, peace and security (hereafter WPS); youth empowerment; ECOWAS standby force; humanitarian assistance; and peace education.

The WPS component is a significant addition to the ECOWAS peace and security architecture. It is the first distinct peace and security provision for women. It strongly suggests that the continued development of the ECOWAS peace and security architecture has occurred within an environment that allows for recognition of the ways in which women can contribute to peace and security. As was the case with earlier provisions for women within ECOWAS, it draws on existing continental and international instruments, including the momentous UN Security Council Resolution 1325 (ECOWAS 2008, paragraph 81). The objective of the WPS component is 'to propel and consolidate women's role and contribution to the centre stage in the design, elaboration, implementation and evaluation of conflict prevention and resolution, and peace-building and humanitarian initiatives while strengthening regional and national mechanisms for the protection and advancement of women' (ECOWAS 2008). This is a comprehensive and well-thought-out agenda that includes women's strategic contribution to the ECOWAS peace and security mechanism in its development, functioning and evaluation. It also recognises the particular needs of women, and the continuing need for their protection.

The WPS component takes the useful approach of promoting

the protection of women through their strategic participation in peace and security processes. For instance, it resolves to review the adequacy of information on the impact of violent conflict on women (thus addressing the issue of women's protection) while recognising and supporting the positive roles played by women in conflict resolution and peace building (ECOWAS 2008: paragraph 82a). This is an inclusive process which prioritises targeted partnerships with women's organisations for research purposes as well as with academic institutions and the private sector for specific training programmes (ECOWAS 2008: paragraphs 82a and 82g).

The significance of women playing key roles in leadership is reinforced by the increasing number of women working on key peace and security issues in decision-making capacities within ECOWAS (ECOWAS 2008: paragraphs 82b and 82c). This is also addressed by proposals for the development and implementation of programmes to improve women's skills base, thereby enabling them to engage in peace and security issues at strategic levels (ECOWAS 2008, paragraphs 82b and 82c). The component also calls on member states to increase the recruitment of women into the armed forces and security agencies as well as into the ECOWAS Standby Force; it does not, however, specify that they should occupy leadership positions (ECOWAS 2008: paragraph 82j).

The WPS component also provides ECOWAS with a vital norm-setting role by committing to the adoption of a sub-regional strategy to address gender-based violence as well as providing policy norms with regard to gender discrimination in all its forms (ECOWAS 2008: paragraphs 82d and 82e). Member states are also called upon to implement the provisions of the component, including the requirement that women should occupy key decision-making roles on peace and security issues (ECOWAS 2008: paragraphs 82h, 82i and 82j).

The department which drives this initiative within ECOWAS is the Department of Gender and Human Development (ECOWAS 2008: paragraph 82a). This is a welcome development, given that it creates the opportunity for the development of a gendered approach to peace and security issues. However, there may be a risk that the engagement of women in peace and security issues will be ghettoised within this department. There is also a risk that this component of ECOWAS will become a catch-all for addressing gender issues as they affect women, thereby losing sight of its specific focus on peace and security issues.

Discussions on the role of women rightly feature in some areas of the ECPF outside of the WPS component. These include early warning, preventive diplomacy, democracy and political governance, human rights and cross-border initiatives. Women's organisations are cited as being significant for the development of sub-regional early warning systems and for the development of preventive diplomacy (ECOWAS 2008: paragraphs 44, 49l and 51f). The participation of women in democratic processes is supported, including in decision-making capacities (ECOWAS 2008: paragraph 53d). Human rights and provisions that are cognisant of the gender discrimination that women face are to be adopted and enforced (ECOWAS 2008: paragraph 57a). With regard to cross-border initiatives, special attention is to be paid to crimes that threaten women's livelihoods (ECOWAS 2008: paragraph 69a).

It is conspicuous that women do not feature in discussions within what may be termed the 'hard security' components, including security governance, practical disarmament and the ECOWAS Standby Force. Although women's engagement in peace and security in strategic roles is called for within the WPS component, the absence of corresponding provisions within other key components may undermine that process, particularly in so far as this affects women's strategic involvement. There is a sense in which women's participation within these components is tied to a particular narrative which represents women as 'soft', as victims, as helpful, peacemaking and peace-loving. This is especially in evidence when women feature within the ECPF as mediators, as sources of information, as victims, and as a focus of human rights issues and cross-border initiatives.

Further evidence of this limited understanding of women's engagement is to be found in the youth empowerment component, which makes no distinct reference to women. This reinforces the idea of 'youth' as young men and excludes the important role that women play as part of this socio-political grouping. This points to the need to acknowledge that as a social category, 'women' are a diverse group. Women are also political actors and leaders, although this does not seem to be recognised when it comes to peace and security issues.

Although these challenges exist within the WPS component, some are being addressed within the nascent ECPF plan of action. This creates opportunities for growth and learning within the ECOWAS peace and security structures. For instance, the action plan makes recommendations with regard to ECOWAS departments that should engage on issues with the WPS component in order to help realise its objectives. The following departments are cited as crucial to achieving the objective of increasing the number of women in senior leadership positions in peace and security structures within ECOWAS and member states: the ECOWAS Commission's Human Development and Gender Department, ECOWAS's Gender Development Centre, the ECOWAS Commission's Department of Political Affairs, Peace and Security, and the ECOWAS Commission's Human Resources Department (ECOWAS 2010: 8).

In order to increase interaction between the WPS component and the 'hard security' elements of the ECPF, the action plan recommends the creation of a parliamentary committee to oversee improved linkages between the WPS component and the military and other security components of the ECPF (ECOWAS 2010: 17). With regard to the recruitment of women into the armed forces, the action plan recommends referencing the level of seniority of those recruited as a benchmark for success (ECOWAS 2010: 18). The action plan also specifies that the promotion of girl child education within the component should focus on developing the curriculum on peace and security training (ECOWAS 2010: 36).

Women in peace and security at the ECOWAS Commission

In this section, I place the ECOWAS Commission in the spotlight and examine, at a rudimentary level, the roles that women play (or do not play) in peace and security at strategic decision-making levels. Arguably, the ECPF is in the early stage of implementation – it was adopted as recently as 2008, and its action plan has been developed even more recently – hence one must guard against unrealistic expectations.

Nonetheless, a snapshot of the roles that women currently play in the institution helps to illustrate the journey so far, as well as the journey ahead, and the extent to which the ECPF may be able to drive change.

The ECOWAS Commission is the central institution for policy making and implementation within the ECOWAS system. It comprises seven offices, each headed by a commissioner. Each commission is made up of between two and four departments, each of which is headed by a director.[4] A simple review of the holders of these posts is available on the ECOWAS website (ECOWAS 2010) and reveals the limited role of women in leadership within the commission (ECOWAS 2010). It presents an even starker picture in the area of peace and security. I now review the proportion of these posts – commissioners and directors – that are held by women in the ECOWAS Commission.

Only two of seven offices – the Office of the Commissioner for Administration and Finance and Office of the Commissioner for Gender and Human Development – have any women in senior positions. In both cases the commissioners are women. This is a pattern worth noting. It could be argued that the Office of the Commissioner for Administration and Finance manages the support services for the ECOWAS Commission as a whole, and that this does not simply constitute a policymaking arm of the commission. Although the office is a vital one, its impact on policymaking and implementation in the sub-region is arguably less than that of other offices.

The Office of the Commissioner for Gender and Human Development addresses policymaking and implementation. However, it is directly engaged with addressing women's issues by tackling the gender imbalances that women face in all aspects of their lives. In the core office dealing directly with peace and security issues – the Office of the Commissioner for Political Affairs, Peace and Security – there are no women at commissioner level or in the four departments/units of this commission. This is especially troubling for the ECOWAS agenda of situating women strategically in peace and security structures in the region. Even within the department that should be driving this, there seems to be a 'ghettoising' of women. This limits the space in which women can engage strategically in policy formulation within the ECOWAS Commission.

This admittedly superficial exercise has not charted changes;

it has simply taken a snapshot of the current leadership within the ECOWAS Commission to illustrate the level of women's participation in senior decision-making roles in the pivotal work that is carried out by the commission. It is likely that since this study was conducted any changes will have been for the better. This is nevertheless a desolate picture: although women comprise at least half the population of the sub-region, only 2 per cent[5] of women are in leadership positions at commissioner level and 0.06 per cent[6] of women are in leadership positions at director level within the ECOWAS Commission – on issues that affect women in very particular ways. The situation is even worse when one looks specifically at peace and security, and in particular at the Office of the Commissioner for Political Affairs, Peace and Security. The dire lack of representation of women in any leadership capacity is likely to undermine ECOWAS's own attempts to push for change in member states. It is failing to fulfil its essential norm-setting role.

Much to celebrate

It was not until ECOWAS was forced to address the reality of internal conflicts in member states that it stumbled on its goal of becoming an ECOWAS of the people. It is through understanding the dynamics of internal conflicts and the challenges faced by citizens of the member states that women have slowly emerged as a group to be taken into account with regard to peace and security issues. The journey has been long. Within the ECOWAS security architecture these improvements are mirrored (at least nominally) in the development of its ECPF with a WPS component and an attendant action plan to actualise the objectives of the component. The ECPF also signifies the culmination of ECOWAS's efforts to develop processes that deal with the root causes of conflict and to actively prevent its occurrence/recurrence.

There is much to celebrate in the ECOWAS approach of redefining security and incorporating a broader constituency in its peace and security agenda. The methodology has been one of constant learning and this has challenged the notion that international organisations are unwieldy and slow to respond. It has also demonstrated the importance of prioritising and utilising local knowledge bases and expertise in policymaking and implementation with regard to peace and security, as well as the need to provide for the protection of women and, eventually, encourage them to come forward as active role-players.

Nevertheless, problems emerge as part of this process. This is apparent when one looks at the rightly celebrated ECPF. The absence of women's voices in peace and security structures within ECOWAS has been noted in my discussion of the objectives of the WPS component of the ECPF: there is an obvious need to increase the number of women in leadership roles in peace and security structures within ECOWAS. It may be argued that it is too early to test the ECOWAS commitment to the WPS component, given that it was only adopted in January 2008. However, assessing the current situation enables one to understand the nature of the challenge and hence to chart a way forward.

The picture is bleak: no women are employed in senior roles within the ECOWAS Commission on governance and peace and security, or within the Office of the Commissioner for Political Affairs, Peace and Security. There is an apparent ghettoising of women's issues to the realm of women, peace and security. This limits the opportunity for women to engage with and assist the functioning of other components of the ECPF. This reality undermines the strength of women's narratives that have helped to place women on the peace and security agenda.

ECOWAS staff members are nominated by ECOWAS member states, so this pattern speaks to deeper structural issues at the level of member-state governments. This underlines the inter-relationship between systems at the national and regional levels. Although ECOWAS continues to play a key role through its norm-setting function it must struggle to overcome these challenges to the representation of women at the strategic level and set the tone for reform.

One of the priorities that emerges in this chapter is the need for ECOWAS to actively seek the promotion of women to strategic roles in order to realise the ideals that it has set itself, and this applies to the ECPF in particular. Ebo (forthcoming) has noted that the ECOWAS Commission does not have a quota system for the recruitment of women. Such a system would necessarily compel member states to fulfil this policy requirement. The aim is to arrive at a point where both men and women adopt gendered approaches in their analysis and therefore also in policymaking and the implementation of peace and security initiatives. Increased representation of women in key strategic positions would enhance this process as their participation would introduce the particularity of their lived experiences and expertise, thereby enabling a fuller understanding of security concerns and needs of society as a whole.

There are clearly structural issues that relate to the way in which gendered roles affect women's strategic engagement with peace and security structures. These include a lack of relevant expertise, poor access to education, the heavy burden of care and household commitments, and the bias against women within the armed forces and security services. Nevertheless, there is clearly scope for ECOWAS to tackle this immense challenge through the use of its normative framework, particularly in the development of its ECPF action plan, as well as through the use of international instruments, such as the provisions of UN Security Council Resolution 1325.

Notes

1. This related to the ECOWAS Protocol on Mutual Assistance on Defence, 1981, Article 4, although it made extensive reference to the role of externals in engineering such internal conflicts.
2. General Okonkwo is a retired major general in the Nigerian army and former force commander of the ECOWAS Mission in Liberia (ECOMIL).
3. President Ibn Chambas began his tenure as the executive secretary of the ECOWAS Secretariat; upon its transformation to the ECOWAS Commission he became the president of the ECOWAS Commission.
4. The Office of the Commissioner for Administration and Finance houses the Administration and General Services Department; Human Resources Department; Conference Department; and Finance Department. The Office of the Commissioner for Agriculture, Environment and Water Resources, hosts the Agricultural Development Department and the Environment and Water Resources Department. The Office of the Commissioner for Human Development and Gender houses the Education, Culture, Science and Technology Department, Gender, Youth, Civil Society Organisations, Employment and Drug Control Department and the Humanitarian and Social Affairs Department. The Office of the Commissioner for Infrastructure comprises the Transport and Telecommunication Department as well as the Energy Department. The Office of the Commissioner for Macroeconomics hosts the Private Sector Development Department, the Research and Statistics Department and the Multilateral Surveillance Department. The

Office of the Commissioner for Trade, Customs and Free Movement hosts the Movement of Persons Department, the Trade, Customs and Tourism Department and the Industry and Mines Department. The Office of the Commissioner for Political Affairs, Peace and Security comprises the Political Affairs Department, Early Warning/Observation Monitoring Centre and the Peacekeeping and Security Department.

5. At the level of commissioner there is only one female commissioner (Office of the Commissioner for Gender and Human Development) in a policymaking capacity, of a total of six commissioners (not including the office of the Commissioner for Administration and Finance).

6. At the level of director there is only one female director (Gender, Youth, Civil Society Organisations, Employment and Drug Control Department) in a policymaking capacity, of a total of 16 departments (not including departments in the Office of the Commissioner for Administration and Finance).

References

Adeniji, O. (1997) 'Mechanisms for conflict management in West Africa: politics of harmonization', *Journal of Humanitarian Assistance*, http://www.jha.ac/articles/a027.htm, accessed 14 February 2010

Cain, K. (1999) 'The rape of Dinah: human rights, civil war in Liberia', *Human Rights Quarterly*, vol. 21, no. 2, pp. 265–307

Ebo, A. (forthcoming) 'The gender dimensions of the ECOWAS peace and security architecture: a regional perspective on UN Resolution 1325', in Olonisakin, F., Barnes, K. and Ikpe, E. (eds) *Women Peace and Security: Translating Policy into Practice*, London, Routledge

Economic Community of West African States (ECOWAS) (1975) ECOWAS Treaty of Lagos, http://www.afrimap.org/english/images/treaty/ECOWAS%20Treaty.pdf, accessed 16 March 2010

Economic Community of West African States (ECOWAS) (1978) ECOWAS Protocol on Non-Aggression, http://168.96.200.17/ar/libros/iss/pdfs/ecowas/14ProtNonAggre.pdf, accessed 17 March 2010

Economic Community of West African States (ECOWAS) (1981) ECOWAS Protocol Relating to Mutual Assistance of Defence, http://168.96.200.17/ar/libros/iss/pdfs/ecowas/13ProtMutualDefAss.pdf, accessed 19 March 2010

Economic Community of West African States (ECOWAS) (1991) ECOWAS Declaration of Political Principlesn, http://www.afrimap.org/english/images/treaty/file423b0220808e6.pdf, accessed 19 March 2010

Economic Community of West African States (ECOWAS) (1999) ECOWAS Protocol Relating to the Mechanisnm for Conflict Prevention, Resolution, Peacekeeping and Security, http://www.sec.ecowas.int/sitecedeao/english/ap101299.htm, accessed 20 March 2010

Economic Community of West African States (ECOWAS) (2001) ECOWAS Protocol on Democracy and Good Governance, http://www.comm.ecowas.int/sec/en/protocoles/Protocol%20on%20good-governance-and-democracy-rev-5EN.pdf, accessed 20 March 2010

Economic Community of West African States (ECOWAS) (2008) ECOWAS Conflict Prevention Framework (ECPF), Abuja, ECOWAS

Economic Community of West African States (ECOWAS) (2010) Draft ECOWAS Conflict Prevention Framework Action Plan – Women, Peace and Security, Abuja, ECOWAS

Ero, C. (1995) 'ECOWAS and the subregional peacekeeping in Liberia', *Journal of Humanitarian Assistance*, http://www.jha.ac/articles/a005.htm, accessed 10 February 2010

Kabia, J. (2009) *Humanitarian Assistance and Conflict Resolution in West Africa: from ECOMOG to ECOMIL*, Aldershot, Ashgate

Keller, E.J. (1996) 'Structure, agency and political liberalization in Africa', *African Journal of Political Science*, vol. 1, no. 2, pp. 202–16

Okonkwo, F. (2008) 'Protection of women civilians in practice: operational case study 1: Liberia', paper presented at Wilton Park conference 'Women targeted or affected by armed conflict: what role for military peacekeepers?', May

Olonisakin, F. (2009) 'ECOWAS and civil society movements in West Africa', *IDS Bulletin* 40, no. 2

Olonisakin, F. and Levitt, J. (1999) 'Regional security and the challenges of democratization in Africa: the case of ECOWAS and SADC', *Cambridge Review of International Affairs*, vol. 13, no. 1, pp. 66–78

United Nations (UN) (1993) The Report of the Secretary-General on the Question of Liberia, UN Doc. S/25402, New York, UN

8

The African Union and security governance

Tim Murithi

Introduction

In this chapter I assess the extent to which the security governance architecture of the African Union (AU) has articulated a
gender dimension. An in-depth description of this architecture
forms the core of the chapter. I assess the efforts that the AU has
undertaken to mainstream gender into its security governance
institutions and agenda and examine how the AU aims to employ
these structures to deliver gender equity. I argue that the AU
security governance process and frameworks have been largely
top–down and that the organisation needs to take more concrete
steps to actualise its normative claims. Specifically, I consider
some illustrations of the limited impact of the AU's norms on its
member states, as a result of the lack of an explicit commitment
to implement initiatives to address gender concerns. Finally, I
propose how to further entrench gender mainstreaming into the
work of the AU's security governance initiatives.

In particular, I consider how Africa has witnessed the conflu-
ence of gender, violence and war in the Democratic Republic of
Congo (DRC) and Darfur. I assess some of the key international
instruments for promoting gender equality, with a specific focus
on United Nations Security Council (UNSC) Resolution 1325,
which stipulates the role that women should play in promoting
security. The chapter will assess how UNSC Resolution 1325
informed the AU's own declaration on gender equality.

AU security governance and gender-based violence

The prevalence of gender-based violence and the use of rape in particular as an instrument of war continues to be a major challenge on the African continent (Meintjes et al 2001). The AU security governance architecture therefore has to be reoriented to address these concerns. In the ongoing conflict in northern Uganda, it is estimated that thousands of women have been victims of rape (Ochieng 2003). The rape of women and children in the DRC has continued despite the efforts of the transitional national government to fight against sexual violence (Action Alert 2004). The World Health Organisation's Health and Reproduction Programme noted that since the war reignited in August 1998, there have been 25,000 cases of sexual violence recorded in South Kivu Province; 11,350 cases in Maniema Province; 1,625 cases in Goma, the capital of North Kivu Province; and some 3,250 cases in Kalemie, a town in south-eastern DRC. A non-governmental organisation (NGO) working on the ground, Nouvelle Dynamique pour la Jeunesse Feminine, says that for the most part, women who have been victims of rape have been rejected by their communities and many by their husbands. This makes the women reluctant to denounce the crimes that have been committed against them in order to avoid such rejection (Schroeder 2004). The women are left without an adequate support system and on top of this, the possibility of contracting HIV/Aids from infected combatants is relatively high.

In Darfur, sexual and gender-based violence has been an ongoing violation of women's rights since the war begun in 2003. For example, on 30 November 2004 seven female internally displaced people (IDPs), one of whom was pregnant, were attacked by an armed militia group near the Deraij camp, in Southern Darfur. '[T]he seven women and girls were fetching firewood outside the camp where they were reportedly attacked, beaten with guns on their chests and heads, and stripped. The armed militia later took three of them to an abandoned hut where they were raped' (Butegwa 2006). According to Butegwa, 'women and girls are still vulnerable to rape whenever they venture out of the IDP camp in search of water or firewood'. This situation still prevailed in

2008, in the absence of a comprehensive peace agreement between Darfur and the government of Sudan. According to Jame Lindrio Alao, a psychologist with the Amel Centre for Treatment and Rehabilitation of Victims of Torture based in Darfur, 'the majority of the perpetrators are allegedly affiliated directly or indirectly with the Government' (Butegwa 2006). To compound the situation for the victims, rape is not yet recognised as a crime by the national laws of Sudan. Even if a woman claims that she was raped, it is more likely that the charge will be changed to one of assault. In addition, the archaic and discriminatory laws in Sudan require four male witnesses to corroborate the charge of rape.

The AU's security governance architecture therefore needs to adopt a more proactive approach in deal with these issues, because the situation for women and children in all war-affected areas is precarious. As Lucinda Marshall (2004) observes, there is a connection between militarism on the continent and the threat to innocent women and children. According to Marshall (2004: 1), 'the theory of power over an "other" provides the common thread between military campaigns and assaults against women. What this theory says is that it is allowable for a person, ethnic group, government, etc. to get what they want by way of power over an other.' For Marshall (2004: 1), what is observed in most conflict situations is that:

> whether implicitly or explicitly, women are the 'other'. Consequently, it becomes necessary in the eyes of those who seek power over [women] to control and belittle women, and all aspects of womanhood. In many cultures, women are viewed as the possessions of their men. Therefore, when a woman is raped, it is effectively an attack on the manhood of her man. Using this reasoning, women become the targets of war in order to attack the honor of the men of a particular culture, ethnic group or country. For these reasons, rape and other forms of sexual assault against women are always a part of war and conflict. When women are assumed to be possessions that can be attacked, stolen and dishonored, they become a means of feminizing and degrading the enemy.

Rape is in effect a war-related crime (Sideris 2001). In this regard, the International Criminal Court (ICC) has also defined acts of sexual and gender violence of all kinds as war crimes. However, progress is yet to be made by the ICC in investigating these crimes and protecting witnesses and victims. Many women in the DRC, Darfur, Somalia and northern Uganda, and victims of previous conflict situations in Sierra Leone and Liberia, are still waiting to see punished those who committed these acts (Twagiramariya 1998). It is therefore vital to consider gender-based violence as a war crime to enforce the necessary international treaties and instruments to ensure the protection of the rights of women and bring perpetrators to justice (Handrahan 2004). In the next section I assess some of these instruments, focusing on instruments established by the UN and AU.

The AU's gender policy framework

The international community has recognised that women are disproportionately victims of the effects of war, yet women have largely been excluded from playing a significant role in making, keeping and building peace. On 20 December 1952 the UN General Assembly adopted the Convention on the Political Rights of Women, which outlined their basic rights of political participation, including the prerogative 'to exercise all public functions, established by national law, on equal terms with men, without any discrimination' (UN 1952). This should include all public functions involved in peace processes within a country. On 18 December 1979 the UN General Assembly adopted the Convention on the Elimination of All Forms of Discrimination Against Women, which provides 'the basis for realising equality between women and men through ensuring women's equal access to, and equal access to opportunities in, political and public life' (UN 1979). Countries that have signed up to the convention are legally bound to put its provisions into practice.

The United Nations took peace and security processes further with the issuing of the UNSC Resolution 1265 on the Protection of Civilians in Armed Conflict on 17 September 1999, which emphasised 'the importance of including in the mandates of peacemaking, peacekeeping and peacebuilding operations special and assistance provisions for groups requiring particular attention, including women' (UNSC 1999: 13). It also asked the secretary-general to ensure that UN personnel involved in peace operations had the necessary training in 'gender-related provisions' (UNSC 1999: 14). On 31 October 2000 the UN Security Council passed its landmark Resolution 1325 on Women, Peace and Security, which specifically reaffirmed 'the important role of women in the prevention and resolution of conflicts and in peacebuilding and ... the importance of their equal participation and full involvement in all efforts for the maintenance and promotion of peace and security' (UNSC 2000). Significantly, this document explicitly codified the universal responsibility of all member states of the UN to ensure that gender issues were mainstreamed in peace and security efforts around the world. UNSC Resolution 1325 also explicitly recommends 'the urgent need to mainstream a gender perspective into peacekeeping operations', as well as the necessity to provide 'Member States [with] training guidelines and materials on the protection, rights and the particular needs of women, as well as on the importance of involving women in all peacekeeping and peacebuilding measures' (UNSC 2000: 6).

These requirements lay the foundation for security governance initiatives by regional and sub-regional organisations such as the AU, which adopted its own home-grown declaration on gender equality and its own gender policy framework. Article 4 (l) of the Constitutive Act of the AU, which formally established the organisation in 2002, adopted as one of its principles 'the promotion of gender equality' (AU 2000). However, it was only two years later, in 2004, that the AU held its first debate on gender issues at its annual assembly of heads of state and government. A number of NGOs lobbied the AU behind the scenes to take a position on gender equality, coordinated by the Senegalese-based women's Femmes Africa Solidarité (FAS) and the Kenyan-based African Women's Development and Communications Network. Their work turned out to be a productive and transformative civil society partnership with the AU (Wendoh and Wallace 2005) and laid the foundation for the assembly of heads of state and government to adopt the Solemn Declaration on Gender Equality (AU 2004). This notes that 'while women and children bear the brunt of conflicts and internal displacement, including rapes and killings, they are largely excluded from conflict prevention, peace negotiations and peacebuilding process in spite of African women's experience in peacebuilding' (AU 2004). The declaration states that the AU will actively work to accelerate the implementation of gender equality in all of its activities. Specifically, it emphasises that the AU would 'ensure the full and effective participation and representation of women in peace processes including the prevention, resolution, management of conflicts and post-conflict reconstruction in Africa as stipulated in UN Resolution 1325' (AU 2004: 2). In addition, it commits the member states of the AU to 'initiate, launch and engage within two years (of the signing of the Declaration) sustained public campaigns against gender-based violence' (AU 2004: 4). The declaration also commits the organisation to implementing legislation to enable women to own land and inherit property, improve literacy among women, and generally mainstream gender parity in all of its social, economic and political activities.

The AU has also recognised the importance of upholding the rights of women's through its Protocol to the African Charter of Human and People's Rights Relating to the Rights of Women in Africa, which was adopted on 11 July 2003 at the AU summit in Maputo, Mozambique. Specifically, the protocol states that 'women have a right to peaceful existence and the right to participate in the promotion and maintenance of peace' (AU 2003: Article 10). It also calls on the member states of the AU to 'take all appropriate measures to ensure the increased participation of women ... in programmes of education for peace and a culture of peace' (AU 2003: Article 10, 2a) and on 'state parties to undertake to respect and ensure respect for rules of international humanitarian law applicable in armed conflict situations which affect the population, particularly women' (AU 2003: Article 10). It further obligates:

> state parties to undertake to protect asylum seeking women, refugees, returnees and internally displaced persons, against all forms of violence, rape and other forms of sexual exploitation, and to ensure that such acts are considered war crimes, genocide and/or crimes against humanity and that their perpetrators are brought to justice before a competent criminal jurisdiction. (African Union 2003: Article 11)

The protocol legislates for equal pay for equal work and establishes affirmative action to foster the equal participation of women in public office. It also legislates against female genital mutilation and promotes medical abortions in specific instances.

Gender and AU security governance

The AU's security governance architecture is predicated on the Protocol Establishing the Peace and Security Council of the AU of 2002, following which, the AU Peace and Security Council (PSC) was established in 2004. The 15-member PSC is mandated to conduct peacemaking, peacekeeping and peace building. The council works in tandem with the chairperson of the African Union Commission and the commissioner in charge of peace and security. The commission is the implementing instrument for decisions made by the PSC to prevent, manage and resolve conflicts. The PSC also assesses potential crisis situations, sends fact-finding missions to trouble spots, and authorises the AU's intervention in internal crisis situations.

The PSC is supported by a continental early warning system on security issues. The military staff committee is composed of defence attachés of the member states of the PSC and provides military advice to the council. In addition, the Panel of the Wise supports the work of the council by initiating its own mediation efforts where the PSC is not involved. To reinforce this provision, the AU is working towards the establishment of an African Standby Force (ASF) by 2010 to cooperate, where appropriate, with the UN and sub-regional African organisations in conducting peace operations. The ASF is to comprise five brigades from west, east, southern, central and north Africa, making the regional economic communities part and parcel of the AU's security governance architecture. The Economic Community of West African States (ECOWAS) is in the process of establishing the ECOWAS ASF brigade. East African countries, including the Intergovernmental Authority on Development, have established a regional mechanism known as EASBRIG Command, which will coordinate the ASF in the east of the continent. In the south, the Southern African Development Community (SADC) is developing the SADC brigade. In central and north Africa regional brigades are being established but at a slower pace.

The AU has also developed a Post-conflict Reconstruction and Development Policy Framework (PCRDPF). Key aspects of this include an attempt to put in place a post-conflict reconstruction system that recognises the importance of an appropriate response to complex emergencies, to social and political transition following conflict, and to long-term development. Therefore, according to the PCRDPF, a post-conflict reconstruction system has at least five dimensions, including: security; political transition, governance and participation; socio-economic development; human rights, justice and reconciliation; and coordination, management and resource mobilisation. In order to maximise the chances of establishing an effective post-conflict reconstruction process, the importance of ensuring that there is a degree of complementarity and mutual reinforcement among these five dimensions needs to be acknowledged. However, it is evident that despite the AU's pronouncements on gender policy, the PCRDPF is not as explicit as it should be about gender mainstreaming in peace-building situations. Ideally, gender policy planning has to be rolled out across the five pillars of the framework as the basis for establishing coherence among the strategies for each area.

The AU's gender mainstreaming initiatives in security governance have been largely top–down and there is a need for it to take more concrete steps to actualise its normative claims. For example, despite the more than five years of its existence, and in view of the numerous policy documents espousing the importance of gender mainstreaming, the PSC has not regularly adopted a gender lens in its work. The council rarely makes reference to ensuring gender equity and promoting gendered decisions on the crisis situations that it assesses. For example, its regular pronouncements on situations in Darfur, Somalia, or the Comoros do not make any explicit references to how the conflict situations are affecting men and women on the ground. The council does not make any reference to the gendered roles of its peacekeepers in the African Union Mission in Somalia (AMISOM) and the AU/UN Joint Hybrid Operation in Darfur (UNAMID), nor to how a gender lens should inform the work of the missions. In March 2010 the PSC convened its first meeting to address the issue of gender mainstreaming, during which it committed itself to convening regular meetings to assess the extent of gender mainstreaming in its work. In terms of the security governance institutional framework to oversee the implementation of these provisions, the chairperson of the AU Commission relies on advice from the AU Women's Committee. As far as the AU's decision-making structures are concerned, the body has adopted a gender parity principle for the composition of the AU Commission, which is the highest executive organ of the Union: five of the ten AU commissioners are, and will be, women. The organisation has also established an AU Directorate for Women, Gender and Development within the office of the chairperson of the commission to oversee the implementation of all of its provisions relating to gender mainstreaming on a range of socio-economic and political issues, including peace and security. The AU has established an African Trust Fund for Women to develop capacity to respond to the union's initiatives on promoting gender equality. The AU still has to genuinely focus on the implementation of these provisions in order to demonstrate its commitment to ending the violent ways in which women are affected by war and are excluded from participating in the promotion of peace and security.

Case studies of gender mainstreaming in security governance

The AU's preventive diplomacy and mediation institution, the Panel of the Wise, is composed of five distinguished elder statesmen and women. The panel is a contemporary rendition of the traditional African institution of the council of elders, but is not a direct or authentic replication in its authority and remit. Specifically, it diverges from the traditional model in that it is partly composed of prominent and distinguished women and has therefore adopted a gender-sensitive reinterpretation of the traditional council of elders, which in the majority of traditional settings was effectively dominated by men. There were, of course, an exceptionally small minority of cultures that ascribed a prominent role to women, particularly in matters of war and peace. The panel's inclusion of women upholds the AU's stated rhetoric on promoting gender sensitivity. It also sends a signal to African societies that women of all backgrounds and levels of expertise are playing a vital role in the promotion of peace on the continent. To date, the panel members have been involved in preventive diplomacy initiatives relating to Somalia, the Central African Republic and South Africa.

In January and February 2008 the then chairman of the AU, former President John Kufuor of Ghana, appointed a former leader of the Mozambican liberation movement, Graça Machel, as a member of the mediation team to respond to the post-electoral violence in Kenya. Machel worked with Kenyan women's networks to ensure Kenyan women played a proactive role in post-conflict peace building in the country (Foundation for Community Development 2008: 3). By adopting such a position, the AU is explicitly stating that the role of women has to become integrated into its security governance architecture. In the case of mediation, women can bring added value to facilitation teams predicated on their vast experience as intermediaries in society. In the Kenyan situation, the opposing mediation teams also had women members.

African civil society has also tried to ensure the implementation of gender mainstreaming in the work of the AU through the Gender Is My Agenda campaign coordinated by a network of NGOs, including FAS (Femmes Africa Solidarité 2005). Initiatives have included a campaign to address the plight of those suffering in the Darfur conflict, particularly women and children. The African Women Consultation on Darfur was convened in January 2008 in Addis Ababa to raise awareness about gender issues, including gender-based violence, in the conflict. The consultation produced the African Women's Declaration on Darfur, which was used in advocacy initiatives at the 2008 AU summit. Indeed, in the margins of the AU summit of that year, approximately 60 women from Darfur lobbied the organisation about their living conditions and the violence that they are confronted with. The AU did not issue a robust statement on Darfur at the summit; however, it referred to its ongoing commitment to resolving the dispute through the initiatives of UNAMID and the efforts of Djibril Bassolé, the Joint UN–AU Special Envoy to Darfur.

Ultimately, however, the weak impact of the AU's norms on its member states is not exclusively a result of a lack of an explicit commitment by the organisation to address gender concerns at the grassroots level.

Moving beyond the rhetoric

On the basis of the declaration on gender equality and the protocol on women's rights, it is evident that in terms of policy and at a theoretical level, the AU has articulated a commitment towards ensuring the well-being of women and the protection of their equal rights. The AU has placed the rights of women at the centre of the continent's security agenda and institutions, recognising that women are key agents in enabling the continent to resolve its multiple conflict situations. However, this policy is yet to be matched by practical initiatives to mainstream gender equality, particularly in security governance (Puechguirbal 2005). Specifically, not all aspects of the declaration on gender equality and the protocol on the rights of women are being upheld and implemented in a systematic manner. Moreover, the reality does not converge with the AU's rhetoric in its declaration and protocol. Specifically, women continue to be excluded from high-level peace negotiations and they are under-represented as AU special envoys to conflict situations. While increasingly more women have been serving in AU peace operations, for example in Darfur, they do not occupy a significant number of leadership positions in these missions. Due to its own internal political dynamics and administrative and bureaucratic inefficiency, the AU is as yet unable to support capacity development for women across the continent. The organisation is therefore no different from other intergovernmental organisations in the lackadaisical approach that it takes to implementing its declarations and protocols.

Even though the AU has adopted the declaration on gender equality and the protocol on women's rights, and five of the organisation's commissioners are women, there is still a reluctance to genuinely bring the key tenets of gender equality into operation, as well as internalise the principles of UNSC Resolution 1325. This is partly due to deeply held cultural beliefs and practices; the fact that the leadership of the AU is composed of men; and the fact that the majority of decision makers at the level of the Assembly of Heads of State and Government, the Executive Council of Ministers and the Permanent Representatives Committee of Ambassadors are still overwhelmingly men. If there is no genuine political will to implement the principles of the solemn declaration and UNSC Resolution 1325, and in the light of the asymmetry in numbers, even the most persistent advocates of gender mainstreaming within these leadership structures, which remain at their core a male fraternity, will find their efforts frustrated (Cockburn 1998). Hudson (1998: 3) suggests that 'most African governments have failed to integrate women into policy formulation, partly as a result of a lack of understanding of gender issues and how to translate these into policy and also because of a reluctance on the part of male power-holders to lose or share deeply entrenched privileges'. The former chair of the AU assembly for 2004–05, the erstwhile President Olusegun Obasanjo of Nigeria, noted that the majority of African countries, like many other parts of the world, still held negative attitudes towards women and excluded them from social, economic and political affairs that affected them. In Africa's current conflict situations, women continue to suffer from the brutality of gender-based violence, and the phenomena of girl soldiers and girl-child sex slaves. In effect, AU gender mainstreaming in security governance processes at the moment does not have a sufficient impact on the lives and concerns of ordinary women on the continent. The AU commission conducted a gender audit of its approach to women's empowerment in its policies and programmes and concluded that management 'needed to do more to achieve the AU's commitments and objectives on gender equality' (African Union 2006: 2). Therefore, it is necessary to shift the focus from viewing policies and legal instruments as the solution to social problems on the continent to analysing the interaction between the policies and the dominant interpretation of social problems.

Gender and the promotion of security governance

The AU Assembly of Heads of State and Government has declared 2010 the Year of Peace and Security in Africa. This declaration is in part designed to encourage African governments and societies to rethink peace and security paradigms. Feminist scholarship should therefore take advantage of this opportunity to reconceptualise how gender mainstreaming can be advanced in the architecture of continental security governance. Through the strategic deployment of the concerns generated by gender-based violence, among other challenges, feminist scholarship can advance policy debates on how security governance systems can be more sensitive to these issues.

Unesco's Statement on Women's Contribution to a Culture of Peace notes that 'only together, women and men in parity and partnership, can we overcome obstacles and inertia, silence and frustration and ensure the insight, political will, creative thinking and concrete actions needed for a global transition from a culture of violence to a culture of peace' (Unesco 1995). In addition, the statement proclaims that 'there can be no lasting peace without development, and no sustainable development without full equality between women and men' (Unesco 1995). According to Koen (2006: 7), 'if women are to play an equal part in security and maintaining peace, they must be empowered politically and economically, and represented adequately at all levels of decision-making: at the pre-conflict stage, during hostilities and at the point of peacekeeping, peacebuilding, reconciliation and reconstruction'. Specifically, 'in times of conflict and the collapse of communities, the role of women should thus be seen as crucial to preserving the social order. Women also have important roles to perform as peace educators in their families and communities' (Koen 2006: 7). The Unesco statement echoes this view when it argues that:

> [w]omen's capacity for leadership must be utilised to the full and to the benefit of all in order to progress towards a culture of peace ... in areas such as conflict prevention, the promotion of cross-cultural dialogue and the redressing of socio-economic injustice, women can be the source of innovative and much needed approaches to peacebuilding.

The Unesco statement recognises that without the active participation of women, it would be impossible to establish any form of durable peace. Women therefore occupy a vital position in achieving the promise of structural peace across the world, and Africa is no exception. Structural peace in this instance refers to the socio-political structures and institutions which are used to maintain and sustain peace. As far as Africa is concerned, women's role in the social dimension of society is not in doubt; however, a significant paradigm and normative shift is needed to ensure that women play a central role in socio-political structures and institutions to ensure that structural peace entrenches itself on the continent (Ekiyor 2004).

Conclusion

In this chapter, I have made the case for the adoption of a gender lens to assess the requirements for security governance in Africa. The fact that women and girls are increasingly the victims of indiscriminate gender-based violence in conflict situations, as evidenced in the DRC and Darfur, suggests that at the very least they should also be agents in the promotion of peace. The international system has issued a range of conventions and resolutions that are unambiguous on the central role that women should play in the political, social and economic life of their countries. The UNSC Resolution 1325 in particular stated the need for women to play more significant roles in peace and security across the world.

I have sought to argue that understanding what security means for women and men and how it can be achieved is central to effective security governance. The AU referred to UNSC Resolution 1325 when it issued its own solemn declaration on gender equality, with its range of recommendations on the role that women should play in promoting peace processes. The AU's protocol on women's rights further outlines vital pan-African legislation to ensure women's active participation in peacemaking activities and their protection from war crimes. However, it is clear that despite the range of AU political and legal statements on gender equality, their implementation has been cosmetic. While there is a gender parity principle that ensures that half of the AU's commissioners will always be women, real changes in the inclusion of women in peace processes are yet to be implemented. Specifically, women continue to be marginalised in peace negotiations, whether as part of AU mediation teams, or special envoys of the union, or even as senior representatives of the delegations of member states. Some commentators have attributed this to the deeply held negative attitudes towards women that are prevalent equally within the security governance institutional structures of the AU and among the governments of its member states. Confronting the impact of gender inequality and continued gender-based insecurity in African societies remains an aspiration rather than a reality. The inclusion of women in peacemaking, peacekeeping and peace-building initiatives would contribute towards redefining gender relations in the promotion of peace and security in Africa. Security governance offers a new avenue to conceptually and practically transform how the AU incorporates a gendered dimension in its policies, initiatives and interventions.

References

Action Alert (2004) *Women's Bodies as a Battleground: Sexual Violence Against Women and Girls During the War in the Democratic Republic of Congo, South Kivu (1996–2003)*, London, Action Alert

African Union (AU) (2000) Constitutive Act of the African Union, Lomé, 11 July

African Union (AU) (2003) Protocol to the African Charter on Human and Peoples' Rights on the Rights of Women in Africa, Maputo, 11 July

African Union (AU) (2004) Solemn Declaration on Gender Equality, AU/Decl.12(III), Addis Ababa, 6–8 July

African Union (AU) (2006) *Chairperson's Second Progress Report on the Implementation of the Solemn Declaration on Gender Equality in Africa*, Addis Ababa, AU

Butegwa, Christine (2006) *The International Criminal Court: A Ray of Hope for the Women of Darfur?*, Kampala, The Darfur Consortium, http://www.pambazuka.org, accessed 20 December 2008

Cockburn, Cynthia (1998) *The Space Between Us: Negotiating Gender and National Identities in Conflict*, London, Zed Books

Ekiyor, Thelma (2004) 'Women's empowerment in peacebuilding: a platform for women's participation in decision making', annual briefing paper, African Women's Development Fund, http://www.awdf.org/awdf/?pid=32&cid=36, accessed 21 December 2008

Femmes Africa Solidarité (2005) *Gender Is My Agenda: Civil Society's Guidelines and Mechanism for the Implementation, Monitoring and Evaluation of the Solemn Declaration on Gender Equality in Africa*, Dakar and Geneva, Femmes Africa Solidarité

Foundation for Community Development (2008) *Implementation of the Solemn Declaration on Gender Equality in Africa: Achievements and Challenges: Drawing Lessons from Mozambique*, Maputo, Foundation for Community Development, 30 April

Handrahan, Lori (2004) 'Conflict, gender, ethnicity and post-conflict reconstruction', *Security Dialogue*, vol. 35

Hudson, Heidi (1998) 'A feminist perspective on human security in Africa',

Caring Security in Africa, monograph 20, Pretoria, Institute for Security Studies.

Koen, Karin (2006) 'Claiming space: reconfiguring women's roles in post-conflict situations', Occasional Paper no. 121, Institute for Security Studies, http://www.iss.co.za/pubs/papers/121/Paper121.htm, accessed 20 December 2008

Marshall, Lucinda (2004) 'Media culpability in the continuum of violence against women', 30 September, http://www.countercurrents.org/gender-marshall300904.htm

Meintjes, Sheila et al (2001) 'There is no aftermath for women', in Meintjes, S., Pillay, A. and Tursen, M. (eds) *The Aftermath: Women in Post-conflict Transformation*, London, Zed Books

Ochieng, Ruth (2003) 'The scars on women's minds and bodies: women's roles in post-conflict reconstruction in Uganda', *Canadian Women Studies*, vol. 22, no. 2

Puechguirbal, Nadine (2005) 'Gender and peacebuilding in Africa: analysis of some structural obstacles', in Rodriguez, Dina and Natukunda-Togboa, Edith (eds) *Gender and Peacebuilding in Africa*, San José, University for Peace

Schroeder, Emily (2004) 'A window of opportunity in the Democratic Republic of the Congo: incorporating a gender perspective in the disarmament, demobilisation and reintegration process', *Peace, Conflict and Development*, vol. 5

Sideris, Tina (2001) 'Rape in war and peace: social context, gender, power and identity', in Meintjes, S., Pillay, A. and Tursen, M. (eds) *The Aftermath: Women in Post-conflict Transformation*, London, Zed Books

Twagiramariya, C. (1998) *What Women do in Wartime: Gender and Conflict in Africa*, London, Zed Books

United Nations (UN) (1952) Convention on the Political Rights of Women, 20 December, New York: United Nations General Assembly

United Nations (UN) (1979), Convention on the Elimination of All Forms of Discrimination Against Women, 18 December, New York, United Nations General Assembly

Unesco (1995) Statement on Women's Contribution to a Culture of Peace, Fourth Conference on Women: Action for Equality, Development and Peace, 4–15 September, Beijing, China

UNSC (United Nations Security Council) (1999) Resolution 1265 on the Protection of Civilians in Armed Conflict, S/RES/1265 (1999), 17 September, New York, United Nations Security Council

United Nations Security Council (UNSC) (2000) Resolution 1325 on women, peace and security, S/RES/1325 (2000), 31 October, New York, United Nations Security Council

Wendoh, Senoria and Wallace, Tina (2005) 'Re-thinking gender mainstreaming in African NGO's and communities', in Porter, Fenella and Sweetman, Caroline (eds) *Mainstreaming Gender in Development: A Critical Review*, United Kingdom, Oxfam GB

Conclusion

Awino Okech

Security as a normative principle and as an expectation from the state by citizens continues in principle to form part of democracy and governance frameworks in Africa. These expectations are not simply about the state's ability to secure its borders from external aggressors and as a result securing its citizens but are also about providing security on a daily basis for citizens within the state. That security as it has evolved on the continent has traditionally pitted citizens against the state is evident in the ways in which post-colonial African states, in addition to securing borders from external aggressors, are often at war with their own citizens. It is therefore commonplace for citizens' perceptions of the state security apparatus – whether the police, immigration officials or the judiciary – to be framed by suspicion and be seen as working against rather than for the people.

In 'Funmi Olonisakin's view (see Chapter 1), this is informed by the emergence and construction of African security govern-ance models by a range of international actors to the exclusion of non-state actors. She notes that while historical moments within and outside Africa provided opportunities for structural change through the end of colonial rule and the end of the cold war, these moments, despite the transformational potential in the narratives that developed around them, were not seized.

However, the diminishing of civil society space through vari-ous forms of state repression, the preponderance of negotiated democracies and accompanying transitional states, have resulted in a swirl of non-state actors contesting political power and doing so through alternative models of security. The fact that these non-state actors, whether they are vigilante groups or 'war lords', arrogate this space is indicative of a failure by the state to respond to varying security deficits – political, economic and social – in the state and society. However, one constant maintains: the absence of due consideration to women's security needs and the opportunities to transform the accompanying gender inequalities.

The movements that emerge to contest state failure have little chance of succeeding, since they tap into a gap within a system but do not necessarily work to transform that structure. Movements that frame their approaches primarily as social justice concerns as opposed to those seeking social justice by claiming political power therefore remain on the periphery. It is perhaps to this domain that the efforts by women's rights bodies have been relegated. Their pursuit of social justice occurs within an existing structure, which is already skewed. In essence their concentration of effort is on inclusion within the state apparatus. Second, since these demands have not been viewed as a pursuit of political power[1] as a means of transformation, they are not challenged nor seen as a threat.

If this is the status quo, and the case studies in this volume have attested as much, increasing attempts to write into a hegemonic narrative that seeks only to include women and not rewrite the narrative is fraught with problems.

The case studies in this volume show how an institutional approach to negotiation while a useful entry point cannot be the only approach. The examples from Sierra Leone and Liberia indicate that these attempts yield gains but not fundamental transformations. Mohammed Sidi Bah (Chapter 5) points to the legal conundrum that prevails in most African states with competing legal regimes, which in effect rather than securing women's rights entrench discrimination. He argues that a constitutional dispensation in Sierra Leone that affirms discrimination while offering a series of new laws to secure women against all forms of violence is not in any way indicative of efforts to take these forms of insecurities seriously but rather maintains gendered structural inequalities. These institutional gains and accompanying inconsistencies are also pointed to in Liberia, with its accelerated programmes to ensure increased enrolment of women in the police force but a lack of targeted efforts to transfer the ethos of the police to other security-enhancing agencies within the state.

Inclusivity or radical shifts?

Olonisakin argued that a crucial indicator for whether a fundamental shift has occured in security governance narratives would be the inclusion of African women and their core concerns. Feminist scholars have consistently argued that militarism, nationalism and colonialism as terrains of power have always been in large part contests over the meanings of manhood (see Dworkin 1997; Enloe 1988; Cockburn 2007). As such, a transformation of these frameworks as organising principles is contingent on the transformation of ideas of manhood and further still gender as a framework that holds currency for social and political organisation. This position does not occlude the multiplicity of roles women play in situations of conflict. Indeed, contexts that give rise to instances of insecurity such as armed conflict lend themselves to redefinitions of dominant masculinities and femininities as has been best documented in Sierra Leone and Liberia (see Coulter 2008). This debate is not what is at issue here. While we are alert to the fact that the opportunities to capitalise on the instability that sexuality as a construct is evident in situations of conflict, the normalisation and return to traditional binaries is almost always instant as the country 'transitions' and how to counter this is of importance.

Olonisakin noted that while there appears to have been a shift at least in definitions, the role and ethos of state security institutions has hardly changed, neither has the purpose for which they were created nor the rules governing their functioning undergone any transformation. The trajectory mapped by Comfort Ero (Chapter 2), Ecoma Alaga (Chapter 4) and Bah affirm that while there has been an emergence of new actors there has not necessarily been a shift in their gendered considerations. The visibility and presence of women as key actors, defining the transformation of these new contexts, remains minimal. The net effect is that in most of the transitioning countries sampled in this book there have been complete reversals of seeming gains made during and in the aftermath of conflict (see Alaga). Ero, while drawing on a tradition of feminist scholarship that has alluded to the potential of transitioning moments as potentially transformative due to the destabilising conditions, is also quick to point out that empirical data that hints at major structural shifts remains minimal. In fact, scholars such as Lydiah Bosire (2006) assert that a constant feature of most of these contexts is the recycling of old actors as new actors. Hence the idea that these countries are in transition can at best be contested.

Our aim in this volume was to establish the ways in which opportunities to rethink structural inequalities can be maintained post-transition. To do so would offer a chance to redefine security as a lived and conceptual terrain, one that takes full cognisance of the gendered realities on the one hand but also offers opportunities for the re-imagining of structural inequalities. The verdict emerging is mixed with three distinct approaches.

There are those that see international instruments as opportunities to localise and adapt 'international clout' as a means to foster local change. Of note is UNSC Resolution 1325 through its provisions for the inclusion of women in peace-building efforts, increase in their numbers in relevant leadership positions as well as their presence in peacekeeping missions. This approach pursued by Eka Ikpe (Chapter 7) and affirmed by Bah and Alaga, albeit in a hybrid version, is timely given the approach of the 10-year anniversary of UNSC Resolution 1325 and efforts within the UN to evaluate not only the difference that this resolution has made in transitioning contexts but also to develop indicators and accompanying action plans for resourcing.

The second hybrid approach acknowledges the value of international instruments as opportunities to negotiate change but recognises that these cannot be to the detriment of local knowledge and realities. The settings that Bah and Alaga describe, Sierra Leone and Liberia respectively, call for the need to institutionalise and learn from tried and tested mechanisms for organising. The imperative of local ownership is stressed even within the opportunities offered through the Year for Peace and Security as framed by Tim Murithi.

The third approach calls for conceptual reconsiderations, emphasising that state and non-state actors charged with taking up 'security' provision are 'irrational'; as such, approaches to engaging with them have to shift. The case from Mozambique highlights that inclusion is not enough, in a context that is perceived to have successfully transitioned without external interference. However, even with the presence of enabling legislation and women in parliament, a situation in which violent gendered narratives continue unabated points to the sustenance of structural inequalities and the absence of real considerations of women's security within these structures. Ero, in noting what other scholars on transitional justice have highlighted (see Mutua 2008), emphasises that as projects in development, there are opportunities to re-examine the boundaries within which transitions and accompanying change can be managed. This includes the opportunity for transitional justice to centralise redistributive justice as a means to addressing structural inequalities.

A final conceptual consideration questions the reliance on gender (as a framework) as a basis for laying claim to the state and the equitable distribution of said resources. Feminist scholarship has pointed to the malleability and fluidity of gender as a construct, others hinting to it as a performative construct, hence not fixed (see Butler 1990; Rubin 1984). Butler and others highlight the importance of gender for what it offers as an explanatory basis for understanding the structure of society but do not necessarily place it at the centre of what will drive a transformative agenda due to its limitations as a framework. Recognising the fluidity of the idea of gender as a construct and accompanying identities in real terms means destabilising the power associated with femininity and masculinity as poles from which power is defined and redistributed. This requires a move away from naturalised, and indeed nationalised, bases of power as constructed through women's bodies as reproducers and producers and as competing sites of disempowerment.

These are important questions, posed and answered in a number of chapters in this volume, by scholars and practitioners who are actively involved in translating the ideals of security governance into a more usable reality. As the case studies demonstrate, the translation of the will to build a secure political community out of a violent past and often continuing reality is fraught with complexities. This volume written by a Pan-African group of scholars and practitioners presents a modest contribution to supporting such efforts.

Note

1. I distinguish here the efforts to increase women's participation in governance systems from a concerted approach to seizing political power, which has not happened in Africa thus far.

References

Bosire, Lydiah (2006) *Overpromised, Underdelivered: Transitional Justice in Sub-Saharan Africa*, http://wwwictjorg/static/Africa/Subsahara/AfricaTJ3. pdf, accessed 19 May 2010

Butler, Judith (1990) *Gender Trouble: Feminism and the Subversion of Identity*, New York, Routledge

Cockburn, Cynthia (2007) *From Where We Stand: War, Women's Activism and Feminist Analysis*, London, Zed Press

Coulter, Chris (2008) 'Female fighters in the Sierra Leone war: challenging the assumptions?', *Feminist Review*, vol. 88, pp. 54–73

Dworkin, Andrea (1997) *Life and Death: Unapologetic Writings on the Continuing War Against Women*, London, Virago

Enloe, Cynthia (1988) *Does Khaki Become You? The Militarization of Women's Lives*, London, Pandora Press

Mutua, Makau (2008) 'Interrogating transitional justice: sexual and gender based violence', in *Unfinished Business: Transitional Justice and Women's Rights in Africa*, Nairobi, ACORD

Rubin, Gayle (1984) 'Thinking sex: notes for a radical theory of the politics of sexuality', in Carole, Vance (ed) *Pleasure and Danger: Exploring Female Sexuality*, Boston, Routledge

Contributors

Ecoma Alaga is co-founder and currently the director of programmes of the Women Peace and Security Network Africa (WIPSEN-Africa), a Pan-African non-governmental organisation based in Accra, Ghana.

Mohamed Sidi Bah is a senior research fellow in the Sierra Leone Agricultural and Research Institute (SLARI) and an independent expert on displacement, reparations and programme evaluation.

Comfort Ero is the director of the South Africa office of the International Centre for Transitional Justice (ICTJ) and the deputy director of ICTJ's Africa programme.

Eka Ikpe is a research associate with the Conflict, Security and Development Group at King's College London.

Tim Murithi is head of the Transitional Justice in Africa programme at the Institute for Justice and Reconciliation, in Cape Town, South Africa.

Benilde Nhalevilo is an independent gender activist with extensive experience working in women's rights in Mozambique.

Awino Okech is a doctoral fellow and lecturer with the African Gender Institute at the University of Cape Town.

'Funmi Olonisakin is the director of the Conflict, Security and Development Group (CSDG) at King's College London. In this role she initiated the establishment of the African Leadership Centre (ALC), which aims to build the next generation of African scholars generating cutting-edge knowledge on peace, security and development.

Helen Scanlon is the director of the Africa Gender Justice programme of the International Centre for Transitional Justice.

Index